CONTENTS

ACKNOWLEDGMENTS

This book started as a conversation with the incomparable Lois Bridges and would not exist without her kind, intelligent, and nurturing comments. Indeed, sometimes it felt like I was writing the book just for her. Though she lives a continent away, her lightning-fast e-mails at all hours of the day and night, her wisdom and sweet encouragement have been the spark and the fuel. I cherish our continuing friendship.

The brilliant Gloria Pipkin provided inspiration and direction at key points in this project. I am grateful for her wisdom and all she has done to help literacy teachers.

The indomitable Amy Rowe worked all hours of the day and night to assemble art charts, pursue permissions, and painstakingly prepare the manuscript for production; no detail escaped her notice.

Dana Truby was the best production editor any author could ask for. She grasped the heart and soul of the book and found the right body to put them in. Thanks to Sarah Morrow for the elegant design.

Brian LaRossa did a marvelous job of capturing the spirit of the book with the perfect Dr. Quantum–like cover and cartoons. I am grateful for his creative spirit, care, and vision. Thanks to Joe Kohl, whose drawings brought my cartoons to life.

Thanks to Terry Cooper at Scholastic for taking a chance on a unique kind of professional book project. Her dedication to real professional development, at a time when quick fixes abound, is inspiring. Ray Coutu offered needed encouragement and creative problem solving.

Thanks to Ann Dumaresq for copyediting and general wisdom. You will always be my comma queen.

Miles Bodimeade, my writing buddy in England, helped with drawings and inspiration in between writing for the BBC. I am grateful for our friendship. Cheers, mate!

Thanks to Gretchen Bernabei for ideas in Chapters 4, 9, and 10. Our lasting friendship in the pursuit of literacy instruction has been one of the greatest joys of my career.

Thanks to Carol Glynn for her ideas on kinesthetic learning. I see your big spirit that fills every auditorium you enter.

The prescient Maja Wilson floated into this book in the final stages when I did a workshop at her school in Ludington, Michigan. Her incisive thoughts on writing rubrics got me thinking deeper about how they work and greatly improved Chapter 9.

The quirky Cathy Campbell made me laugh till the gerunds fell out of my ears. You are the giggliest grammar teacher I know.

The most wonderful Joyce Kohfeldt first told me the story of Ellison Onizuka, and this book goes to press on the 20th anniversary of the first space shuttle disaster, in which he died. I hope Joyce's story honors his great spirit: *Mahalo nui loa.*

To Judy, Larry, Tracy Kendall, and Linda Biehl—what can I say? I was so honored to be part of the Amy Biehl Foundation and the work you continue to do in the new South Africa.

Betty Melburg and Pat Eastman, the best book reps in the Wild West, gave me useful marketing direction along the way. It's great to see sales reps who have a vision for real professional development. Like the best teachers, you spread the seeds that help children grow. We salute all you do for children.

Thanks to my daughter Jessie for helping design the cover and for helping me find the time to finish a chapter or two while we hung out at the camp in Maine. Her patience with a father who lives too much in his head is much appreciated. Thanks to Gracie, who made space in her life for me to write another book. I am so proud to be your father.

As always, my wife, Carol-lee, is the source of all that's good and lasting in my life. Our spontaneous conversations and constant companionship inspire me to be a better person. I am so grateful.

TEACHING WITH YOUR HEART AND SOUL

Here I am standing with Todd Kraai, principal of New Era Elementary School in New Era, Michigan. Mr Kraai believes that the only way to improve schools is if all adults in the school give generously of their time to every student and teach all students to know that they are special. He also believes that learning should be fun and

> A teacher affects eternity; he can never tell where his influence stops.
>
> —*Henry Brooks Adams*

engaging and that he and his teachers must model everything they want their students to do on a daily basis. If you go to New Era Elementary School, you will see Mr. Kraai standing out in front of the school every morning to greet the sleepy children as they get off the buses, as well as every adult who walks into his school. The young children hug him; the older boys give him high fives, ask him what book he is reading, and share their books with him. The teachers nod at Mr. Kraai's welcoming face and know they are safe to teach here. He tells them regularly

Me with Principal Todd Kraai

that there are many ways to accomplish the same goals and encourages their creativity even though he is under great pressure to achieve results. Both the children and the teachers know they can come to him with crazy ideas and he will consider them. In the past few years, he has ridden an elephant around the school, taken the whole school to an indoor water park for the day to celebrate reaching a school goal, and been duct-taped to the wall in the gymnasium by the whole school during a very memorable lesson on adhesion.

You should also know that New Era has been a Golden Apple School and voted one of the five best achieving schools in the state of Michigan.

Creativity, passion, and good humor will always be the motivating forces in learning, but these days it takes another quality to teach effectively: courage. Courage to teach in a way that you know is good for children no matter what you are being told from above; courage to create lessons that break the mold and teach your students to see with their own eyes and hear with their own ears; courage to see that you don't always have to follow the state teaching standards. The standards can follow you.

I wrote *But How Do You Teach Writing?* as a trumpet call to teachers of all grade levels, content-area teachers, and all school administrators. It is not a normal professional development book because its aim is to inspire as much as to teach, to encourage as much as to show how. This book will show you why we teach writing as well as how to teach writing.

The book is divided into three parts. Part I, Out of the Gate, contains concepts and ideas to help you get started teaching writing. Part II, Reasons to Write, shares powerful motivational concepts in fiction and nonfiction writing. Lastly, Part III, Refining Writing, deals with important issues such as revision, grammar, and assessment. Furthermore, each chapter contains mini-lessons titled Try This! for you and your students, and stories and concepts to drive home the points made. Lane's laws of literacy also run through the text and showcase truths I've learned over the years about language and literacy and teaching and learning. At the end of each chapter is a "Yeah, But. . ." section where I tried to address concerns I have collected from teachers of all grade levels around the country. If you have additional concerns, I invite you to e-mail me your "Yeah, But . . ." questions at barry@discoverwriting.com. I will do my best to find you an answer and refer you to resources.

Miss Foley

At right is Miss Foley, my wonderful fourth-grade teacher. She was my Great One, the teacher who turned the sad, tortured third grader who walked into her classroom in September into a fluent writer by May. I am not going to tell you how she did it now, but by the end of this book you will know. I will tell you that Miss Foley, like so many great teachers, took control of her curriculum and taught in a way that she thought was best for her students. She also brought her passions into the classroom and taught with her heart on her sleeve, even though, in the '60s, she felt many of the same pressures to conform to the curriculum standards and meet textbook demands that teachers endure today.

A few years ago, I wrote a song about Miss Foley. You can see me sing it on my YouTube channel (barrylane55). It's a persuasive essay—the verses of the song describe Miss Foley's classroom, and the chorus describes the public's general response to teachers and what we need to do to improve the situation. My favorite verse of the song is this one:

> Miss Foley never married
> She never had offspring
> Unless you count the 600 she cheered on to sing
> We rarely come to visit her
> We hardly ever write
> But she follows us around each day
> And sits with us each night.

Truly great teaching is not limited to time and space. It lives forever.

I hope that along with giving you many ideas on how to teach writing, this book will give you the courage and permission to teach with your heart and soul—like Todd Kraai and Miss Foley and all the other great ones. Your students deserve the best, and so do you.

PART I

OUT OF THE GATE

Writing is thinking
on paper.

—*William Zinsser*

CHAPTER 1

YOU'RE A WRITER, TEACH WRITING

Reclaiming the Spark of Your Own Literacy

On the next page is a piece of writing I did in third grade. It is a book report, written the day before Open House Night. I can almost hear my teacher crying, "Quick, it's Open House Night. Read a book!" It was jammed into an folder labeled "Open House" and stored in the attic of the garage at my mother's house, next to a stack of bald tires that should have been taken to the dump. The box was taped up with masking tape and said "school stuff" on it.

> I learned that you should feel when writing, not like Lord Byron on a mountaintop, but like a child stringing beads in kindergarten— happy, absorbed, and quietly putting one bead on after another.
>
> —*Brenda Ueland*

Though the handwriting is better than you will find in most classrooms today, there is very little of me in this piece of writing. I write a few lines about what the book is about and then I end with the classic line, "Read the book and find out what happens. Book Report by Barry Lane." I am not entirely sure I even read the book.

That was third grade. In tenth grade it wasn't any better; in fact, it got worse. Teachers just gave up and gave us lists of questions to answer. On the next page is the beginning of my book report on the autobiography of that great American writer, Joe Namath.

The Simpletons book report

Book report on Joe Namath book

Notice how stilted the writing is. This was not the quirky kid I was. I use words straight out of travelogue writing—words like *antics*. But notice what my teachers cared about. Look at the grade. I got a B- and the comment: "It's nice to read typewritten work." Those were the two qualities my teachers cared about when I was in school—grammar and neatness. Those are important qualities of writing, no doubt. I am not saying students should write sloppily or they should write ungrammatically, but you don't hear Oprah gushing, "We chose this book because of the neat margins." Or "This is a fine novel, with not one misspelled word." Readers care about other things: vivid, pertinent detail, honesty, voice, humor, organization, idea development, guts, passion . . . you name it. As readers, we want real stories, essays, and reports, not the "schoolified" writing assignments my seventh-grade teacher Mrs. Kent wanted us to complete.

The one creative assignment we did each week was to put all the spelling words into a paragraph. This would often lead to compelling sentences like, "He abated her so she abashed him." One day my teacher Mrs. Kent made me stay after school and tear my weekly spelling list into little pieces. I had written a parody of the assistant principal's latest speech, but, in my defense, I did manage to work in all the spelling words. In her mind, the reason she made me tear it up was simple: "He might get the wrong idea about the kinds of assignments I am giving."

You see, the concept that students could give themselves an assignment didn't exist. In this book, we are going to learn how to create a class that gives itself assignments. And if you don't teach this way already, you will delight in the joy your students' initiative will bring to your teaching.

Mr. Francis Gray, my eighth-grade teacher, was one of those who delighted in student initiative. Mr. Gray wore gray suits and had gray hair, but nothing else about him was gray. He cared about his subject and he cared about us. He believed in creativity and had us do something he called "the creative project." I'm almost sure he wrote it just like that in his plan book for months. I had written a lot of humor in school, but I would get either a C- or a "See me" for a grade, so I stopped showing it to teachers. I took a chance in Mr. Gray's class and added this poem to my creative project.

'Twas the night before school starts and all through the hut

Not a creature was smoking, not even one butt.

The school clothes were hung

By the chimney on a chair,

With hopes that by morning they would disappear.

My brother in his tee shirt

And, I, in mine, too

Were just getting ready

To enter the blue

When all of the sudden

There came such a roaring.

I knew at that second,

This life wouldn't be boring.

I ran to the window

As fast as a sprinter

And looked at my seat

And found 17 splinters

And what to my wandering eyes should I see then

But a 12 tire, 525 horsepower garbage truck with 5 miniature garbage men.

They said not a word

But went straight to our cans

They hoisted them up with their tired grubby hands

The head driver of the crew yelled at his men
On Harry, on Benny, on Simon and Den.

And I heard them cry out as they rode past a bus
You blankety-blanks stay in school or else you will end up like us.

At the bottom of the page, Mr. Gray wrote, "Excellent parody of The Night Before Christmas." I didn't even know what a parody was, but I was in eighth grade and I had a subscription to *Mad* magazine. Mr. Gray gave credence to forms of writing that were not just school writing. In Chapter 7, we will explore alternative forms of writing and how they can revive report writing in any subject.

Mr. Gray told me I had a talent with words and I should pursue it. He implored me to enter the spring poetry contest. You had to write a poem about the word *if*. Here is my poem.

if

If is a word
that's become very trite.

It's been used through the ages
With no end in sight.

It's been used by peoples
Small and vast,
but mostly by those who live in the past.

An "iffer" believes the world needed no change
He just keeps on singing, "Home on the range"
Although people call him hopeless and strange
He keeps "iffing" and "iffing" the world hadn't changed.

And so the "iffer" ends his stay.
Sad and disappointed he goes on his way.
His life has been one big myth,
All because of the little word *if*.

I won the contest and the certificate was presented to me by none other than my seventh-grade teacher, Mrs. Kent (the same one who made me tear up the spelling quiz). No sweeter literary victory was ever won. I can still hear her slightly shaky voice as she nervously handed me the certificate: "And here is a man of many surprises," she said.

They put me in an honors English class, and it took me only a half semester to prove myself unworthy. I wrote haikus like,

> Hard boiled egg yolk
> Why couldn't you be a chicken?
> Who aborted you?

> Television set
> I stare at you constantly
> It's nothing personal.

Soon I was back in the vocational English class. And by the time I left high school this is what I looked like. Have you ever seen a sadder, more irony-deficient face than this one?

Me, in high school

Here's what I looked like 25 years later.

Me, 25 years later

It's taken me years as a writer to get back to where I was in Miss Foley's fourth-grade class. If you want your students to be writers, you need to share your writing with them as I have shared with you. But before you do that, you have to reclaim the spark of your own literacy for yourself. Here's a good place to start.

TRY THIS!

RECLAIMING THE SPARK

1. Get a blank piece of paper.

2. Draw a line down the middle. On one side write "School"; on the other, "Life."

3. List all the writing assignments or work from school that you can remember on the left. Examples might include reports, essays, stories, poems, etc.

4. Brainstorm a list of all the writing assignments from life on the right. Examples might include notes, birthday cards, letters to loved ones, e-mails, cartoons, illustrated stories, etc.

5. Share examples with others to help trigger more ideas. Let your list grow long.

If you are working with a group or study circle, take time to share your memories. This will trigger more assignments to add to the list. If you have a mother or father who saved things, go to their attic and see if you can find old examples of your writing, from school and life.

Debriefing

Is there a pattern to the writing you remember? Was most of the interesting writing done in the home or at school? What assignments stuck with you all these years? Which assignments faded away?

A WRITER TEACHES WRITING

The best advice I've ever heard about teaching writing came from the great Donald M. Murray, who died in December 2006 at the age of 82. Murray, who turned in his last column to *The Boston Globe* three days before his death, always said that we write to find out what we don't know we know.

Donald Murray

Murray won the Pulitzer Prize for editorial writing in 1956, and he divided his time between teaching at the University of New Hampshire and freelance writing. His many books on writing and his generous spirit inspired a whole generation of writing teachers.

This is what Murray often said when anyone asked him how to teach writing. "You're a writer. Teach writing."

But maybe you don't feel like a writer. Here is a way to assess your and your students' attitudes toward writing.

WHEN I WRITE, I . . .

1. Begin with this phrase: "When I write I . . .".

2. Now set a timer for seven minutes and quick-write.

3. Read over and discuss what you wrote with a partner or with the class.

> ### RULES OF QUICK WRITING
>
> - Write fast.
> - Don't cross out.
> - When you get stuck, write your thoughts.

Debriefing

Look over what you wrote. What assumptions can you make about your attitudes toward writing? What is the advantage of quick-writing? What are the disadvantages? How can you use quick-writing as a tool for your instruction?

Look at the example of a fourth grader's quick-write on the next page. What do you notice about the writing?

Maybe you have a good attitude toward writing but you have a critical voice in your head that puts down your writing. This critic might be a teacher from the past or that grammatically zealous friend who red-penciled your letters and sent them back for correction. Here's another way to reclaim your spark.

When I write, I hear a little voice inside my head saying that okay but a little better. So I make it better. Then I come up with more and more idea for my story. I'm stuck here and I don't know what to do so I think I'm going to wait for a minuter. "Tick, tock, tick, tock, tick, tock"

A fourth grader's writing example

TRY THIS!

ROOTING OUT THE VOICES IN THE MARGINS

1. Think back to your career in school and all the comments and tips you remember teachers writing on your papers.

2. Make a list of all those comments or tips.

3. Write about how these comments or tips improve or detract from your attitude toward writing.

Debriefing

What effect did your teachers have by writing on your papers? Did these comments improve the quality of your work? How do you offer criticism to your students?

On the next page is a piece of writing from my sophomore year of high school. I was attempting to write a satire about going to the dentist's office, in a *Dragnet* style. I thought I had captured the staccato tone well until I saw the note in the margin from my teacher.

This teacher obviously did not get the joke. But to her credit, it's hard to know the intent of the writer unless you have time to sit down with him and confer.

When I have done this activity with teachers over the years, I have learned that they can write some pretty painful things on their students' papers. Here are some cutting comments I have collected:

A writing sample from my sophomore year in high school
Teacher's note: "Combine Sentences for a less choppy effect."

- *Trite*
- *A little knowledge is a dangerous thing*
- *Ugh*
- *F: You'll know why in 10 years*

In my thousands of workshops with students and teachers, I have learned that teacher comments can leave scars that don't heal for years. Professional writers know that negative voices can be overcome by lowering their standards. Don Murray once wrote a piece called "The Importance of Writing Badly," in which he suggested that our writing often falls apart when we are trying to express deep emotion or complex ideas. Murray urges us to follow the language like a river and not push our ideas into perfect sentences. Form follows substance. In my first book, *Discovering the Writer Within* (coauthored with Bruce Ballenger), we suggested writing a letter to your watcher, the critic who stands at the gates of your imagination scrutinizing the fruit of your creativity.

TRY THIS!

WRITE A LETTER TO YOUR CRITIC

1. Write the words "Dear Watcher."
2. Write a letter to your Watcher, expressing concerns, asking questions, and so forth.

3. Share your letters and discuss the origin of your watcher and how you can contain its negative qualities.

Debriefing

What is your relationship with your critic? How could it be improved? As you read the example below, think about how we balance critical insight with creative thought.

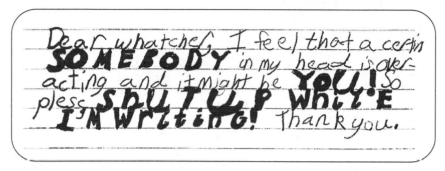

Letter to inner critic from a fourth grader

A NEW WRITING PROGRAM

I want to tell you about a new writing program. It is based on years of experience as a teacher and a student, a wealth of progressive pedagogy, and classroom-proven lessons. This program is creative and flexible enough to fit the needs of all your students. It adapts almost instantly to special-needs students and it comes in different sizes and shapes and colors, all carrying a lifetime guarantee. Unlike most writing programs, this one comes with yearly and monthly supplemental installments that automatically add to its knowledge base, free of charge. It can also spontaneously rewrite daily lesson plans based on ideas occurring in the morning shower or in the car on the way to school.

If you haven't guessed yet, you can view this new program in the nearest mirror. This new writing program is you.

> **LANE'S FIRST LAW OF LITERACY**
>
> No writing program can replace a teacher who creatively adapts
> to the needs of his or her students. Not now. Not ever.

But how do you get started teaching real writing when you have never done it before or when you have curriculum restrictions that limit your time to teach writing? In the next chapter we will begin with a quick assessment of where you are and then get the ball rolling in many different ways. I want to show you not only how easy it is to begin this process but also how enjoyable teaching writing can become for you and your students.

"YEAH, BUT . . ."
Readers' Questions Answered

You know, writing with your students is a great idea in theory, but I spend most of my time helping my first-grade students get started, conferring with them, and so forth. I don't really have time to write with my students.

It is true that your students need you, but your students also need to see you writing with them. Even if you take only seven minutes a day to sit there in front of them struggling to find ideas to write about, you are modeling all the things that make writing important. It also gives you a chance to share your struggles and insecurities about writing with them.

Example:

Me: "You know, I really just don't know what to write about today. Can you guys give me a suggestion?"

Class: "Write about your gerbil again."

Me: "I wrote about him all last week. I want to write about something new."

First-grade students will be drawing their stories along with writing them. You can also do some drawing and talking about how the drawing gives you ideas to write about.

How do I create an excitement for writing when the kids groan every time?

When kids groan at writing time, it's usually a sign that they don't have enough opportunities to choose what they want to write about. They don't see writing time as their time to explore. It is lesson-driven, teacher-driven, and assignment-driven. Escaping this paradigm is the first order of business. Kids need writing notebooks; they need open-ended assignments. "Anything" must become the default subject setting of your writer's workshop. Even great and important lessons on craft cannot replace time when students can explore their own ideas in writing. Save those lessons until after you have the ball rolling. If you write with your students, you will soon find that you, too, look forward to writing time because it is a time for you to reflect, an oasis in the midst of a hectic day. But, realize that at times it will seem like it's not working at all. When this happens, sit back a bit and give them the freedom to write with you. It's okay to help students, but only after they have tried to help themselves.

My watcher is always telling me I will be a better writer when I get a bigger vocabulary. What should I say back to him?

Believe it or not, the words you own are the best words to use in your writing. There is no need to use big words to be a better writer. "Never use a long word when a short one will do," said George Orwell, Mark Twain, William Cullen Bryant, and probably another dozen writers. Abe Lincoln proved in his debates against Stephen Douglas that simple rhetoric and storytelling cut like a razor through fancy, elevated language. Mark Twain is still probably the best example of a writer who used simple country logic and small words to communicate. Twain's most famous creation, Huck Finn, is a moral philosopher, a poet, and an eloquent interpreter of the world. He has never been to school. He is not "book-smart." Like the best writers, he uses the words he owns to speak his truth. Let Huck Finn be your model.

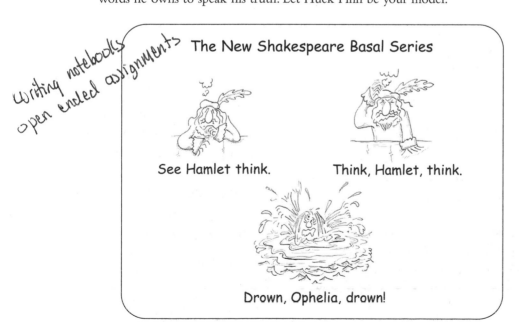

Writing notebooks open ended assignments?

The New Shakespeare Basal Series

See Hamlet think.   Think, Hamlet, think.

Drown, Ophelia, drown!

copyright 2008 Discover Writing Press www.discoverwriting.com

CHAPTER 2

TIME + SPACE + CHOICE = REAL WRITING

Do you have a writing classroom? Take this simple test.

1. After giving a writing assignment, your students . . .

    A. groan

    B. sigh

    C. whine "How long does it have to be?"

    D. say "Yippee!"

2. When you announce it is writing time, students . . .

    A. groan

    B. sigh

    C. say "How many sentences do I have to write?"

    D. say "Yippee!"

3. When you announce there is no time to write today, students . . .

    A. shout "Hooray!"

    B. sigh in relief

    C. say "Yippee!"

    D. throw things at you

> Close the door. Write with no one looking over your shoulder. Don't try to figure out what other people want to hear from you; figure out what you have to say. It's the one and only thing you have to offer.
>
> —*Barbara Kingsolver*

If you answered anything but "D," we need to talk. When students have a negative attitude toward writing, it will always show up in their work. Too many teachers and too many curricular guidelines assume that writing is a set of basic skills learned through daily practice while forgetting the real deal: Writing is thought, writing is expression, writing is about having something to say. This starts very early in life. After all, babies don't learn to talk with textbooks.

Years ago, when I was in college, I had a work-study job at a day care center. There was a 3-year-old whom I will call David. David had been coming there since he was an infant and his vocabulary wasn't growing very quickly. At one of our weekly meetings, one of the workers at the center suggested that David's lack of language stemmed from the fact that we all knew what he wanted when he grunted and pointed. He had developed his own caveman vocabulary with hand gestures and grunting, and we were playing right into it by not demanding that he use words. From then on, we all decided to pretend David was a foreign tourist whenever he asked for something. We pretended not to understand him until he spoke our language, and sure enough, David's vocabulary developed. It developed out of his drive to express his needs.

Expression is the engine of language. Take it out of your classroom and all you have left are empty assignments that are all due on Tuesday. (Make sure you double-space and put your name at the top of the page, please.) Put expression back into your classroom and suddenly the world changes. Students can't wait to write and share what they have written. Plays, poems, essays, stories blossom from their pens, and the assignment due on Tuesday for a grade is no longer the goal—the writing, saying what you have to say, is the goal.

Have you ever noticed that a student's reading level rises in proportion to the interest the child has in the book he or she is reading? The same is true of writing.

LANE'S SECOND LAW OF LITERACY

A strong horse will pull any cart.

I once coordinated a literary project grant for Adult Basic Education of Vermont called "Opening Doors Books." The grant proposal noted the lack of basal reading material available to adult literacy students, which forced them to read children's books that might not interest them. The idea was to have new readers write biographical stories about people like themselves in order to provide more compelling reading, and thereby help them excel. We met in libraries across the state and wrote memoirs at our writing workshops. The

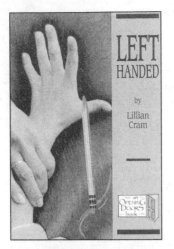

Lillian Cram

stories were distributed and voted on by literacy students throughout the state, and six were chosen to be turned into small chapbooks that were illustrated by professional artists. Each of the six stories, chosen by hundreds of new readers, dealt honestly with difficult and painful subjects. The poet Veranda Porche says, "We write to correct life's unfairness," and from the voting it was clear the same might be said of reading. *The need to make sense of the past fuels language.*

We also chose books for adult literacy students to use. One of the books we chose was *Left Handed* by Lillian Cram. The author describes her experience as a left-handed child in a class in a one-room schoolhouse where writing left handed was forbidden. This misguided practice was common in many schools in years past. Cram describes what it was like to have her left hand tied behind her back and, ultimately, how she confided in her parents, who then came to school to straighten things out. After the book was published to wide acclaim and a review in *The New York Times*, the Adult Basic Education office in Bristol, Vermont, received an envelope containing a crumpled piece of a brown paper bag and a five-dollar bill. Scrawled on the paper, in crayon, was this note: *Send me that book about the left-handed woman right now!*

The woman who scribbled this note had what I call the quintessential literary experience. She read about a stranger's experience and proclaimed to herself, "That's me!" Learning to write is not about acquiring a big vocabulary or using fancy metaphors. Learning to write is about learning to tell the simple truth.

LANE'S THIRD LAW OF LITERACY

The simple truth has enormous power.

The poet Philip Levine gave this law to me. I had written to him to ask if he would be willing to send me a review or two of the six chapbooks for the adult literacy project mentioned above. I had sent the book to other American writers, and they either didn't respond or wouldn't honor my request. My most disappointing response came from a novelist whom I greatly admire. He wrote a short note that concluded with these words, "These are interesting stories but I cannot in good conscience call them literature."

I opened Levine's letter fearing the worst, but I was pleasantly surprised. Levine began with a playful request not to let any of his friends see the blurb, as he had made it a practice never to write blurbs for anybody. But these stories were so strong he just had to respond: "These stories have proven something to me that I have often thought but never said: The simple truth has enormous power."

Five years later, Philip Levine won the National Book Award for a collection of poems. The title was *The Simple Truth*.

So how do you teach your students to write the simple truth, and find their own, unique voices? Where do you start creating a writing classroom based on real thought and not just assignments due on Tuesday? Here is a "mathematical" equation, to get us started.

Time + Space + Choice = Real Writing

I was once working with a group of teachers who chose topics for their students to write about. When I asked what it would be like if they gave their students a choice of what to write, there was a long pause, and then one teacher raised her hand and said, "If I let kids write about what they want to write about, it may take them half an hour just to figure out what to write about. I can't spare a half hour."

Author Donald Graves says if you don't have your elementary students write an hour a day on topics of their own choosing, you are not even teaching writing.

LANE'S FOURTH LAW OF LITERACY

Real writing takes real time.

We need to make time, space, and choice a priority in the classroom. Let's start with time.

TRY THIS!

FINDING THE TIME

Let me tell you what you know already. You don't have enough time to do all the things you are sometimes asked to do as a teacher. Whether you are an elementary school teacher dealing with 25-plus students and six subjects all day or a middle or high school teacher dealing with one subject and hundreds of students, time is not on your side. There is simply not enough of it. So let's think of your day the way the government thinks of a yearly budget, only instead of money, you are budgeting time. You are looking for the best investment.

Below is a list of school days, and beneath each day are eight blocks of time. You may not need all of them. Find at least three blocks you could turn into writing blocks on a regular basis.

If you are a content-area teacher at the upper levels, you may want to devote only a portion of the period to daily writing. For example, a history or science teacher might want to devote the first five minutes or last five minutes of every class.

Experiment with different ways of blocking time. The goal is to create a regular sustained writing time.

Monday	Tuesday	Wednesday	Thursday	Friday

Debriefing

Were you able to find a regular time to write five days a week? What obstacles did you run across? Is it possible to overcome those obstacles? Can you make that writing time a habit in your class?

Create a Regular Writing Time

I remember the first time I really came to see the importance of regular writing time. I had just walked into a second-grade class in a California elementary school. The children were all spread out comfortably around the room writing in their notebooks, lounging across beanbag chairs, reading to each other, scribbling so hard no one even noticed I had walked in. Suddenly, a little boy who had been buried in his writer's notebook looked up at me.

"What are you doing here?" he said with a worried look, "Don't you know it's writing time?"

"I'm a writer," I said. "I am here to do a lesson." He looked up and down, sizing me up.

"I hope you brought your journal," was all he said before turning back to his writing.

When a teacher surprises a class with a writing assignment, students often feel like they are being ambushed. The teacher assumes that writing is like a faucet that, at a moment's notice, can be turned on. This may be true for some students, but most students need time to think. Instead of turning on a faucet, these writers have to cast a big, clumsy wooden pail down into the well. Splash!

A regular and predictable writing time allows students time to rehearse what they are going to write about in their heads, hours before it's time to write. It makes writing more effortless because it is an extension of the thinking that preceded it. Simply put, an elementary school student who makes a daily writing goal in the morning might have all day to think about his story before he actually sits down to write. He

> Writing is long periods of thinking and short periods of writing.
>
> —*Ernest Hemingway*

"Now, freewrite about your deepest, darkest secret."

copyright 2008 Discover Writing Press www.discoverwriting.com

may even be eager to write down the thoughts that have been circling in his brain. At the high school level in the content areas, a writing block can be a predictable time to make personal connections and ask probing questions about the material being studied.

But the most important reason for a regular writing time is that the teacher no longer has to tell students to write. After all, it's writing time. Get with the program. Put on your writing hats.

But What About the Writing Process?

When teachers began teaching the writing process to their students, it was an attempt to define the stages of writing in order to help writers know where they are and where they are going.

What went wrong with writing process?

copyright 2008 Discover Writing Press www.discoverwriting.com

The Writing Process

- Brainstorm
- Web
- Draft
- Revise
- Edit
- Publish

At first, it was a great improvement over teaching that presumed writing emerged magically from a student's pen, but like all good ideas in education, over time it became as much a burden as a help to writers. Some teachers insisted that all students go through all the stages of the writing process for each piece of writing. Textbooks and state curriculums often insisted that students follow each stage religiously. Students groaned, *Can't we just write?*

Fear not. There is no need to abandon the writing process, but we need to see it in a different light. Let's view the writing process not as lockstep stages but as a set of writing tools.

Prewriting strategies like webbing (graphic organizing) or brainstorming can be useful to some writers, but not all writers. Drafting and editing are tools all writers might use, but at different stages of their own unique writing process. I might be the kind of writer who starts by drafting and skips prewriting, or the kind of writer who doesn't draft until I have a firm idea of where I am going. Furthermore, I may decide, after I have finished a story, to web or brainstorm in order to find a good title. Or maybe I am the kind of writer who can't write a single word until I have a working title. All writers have their own writing process with their own tools and stages.

Take a minute now to look at your own and your students' writing process.

TRY THIS!

MY WRITING PROCESS

Here's an assignment to try with your students. Think of the last time you had to write something, be it a college entrance essay, a letter to the editor, a story or poem. What stages did you go through? Have fun coming up with creative, out-of-the-ordinary stages. For example, instead of free writing I may have free staring or free avoiding.

Writing Process

1.

2.

3.

4.

5.

Me practicing free staring

Making the Space for Writing

Once you have cleared some time in your schedule, you may also want to make some space. But how do you make space for writing, and what does it mean? Your classroom is a certain size. You can't make it any bigger. Can't students just write at their desks? Well, yes and no.

Stop for a minute and think about your experience as a college student. Were you the kind of student who wrote all your papers while sitting in a tiny sterile cubicle in the library with a fluorescent light buzzing above you, or were you and your books sprawled out across a sofa at the student union building while you sipped coffee and scratched sentences in your notebook as you gawked at passersby? Most classrooms favor the former, but how can we also make a classroom more comfortable for the latter? Over the years, I have collected suggestions from teachers of all grade levels on ways to make classrooms more comfortable for writing.

Clipboards for each student

Using a clipboard can be like having your own personal portable writing office. I often work with 200 students crammed into a library for a writing workshop. Even if we had enough desks, it wouldn't work as well as it does having a clipboard for each student.

Writing pillows

It's time to write. Get your writing pillow and your clipboard and get to work. The nice thing about a writing pillow is that you take it and your notebook anywhere in the room and create your own instant office. Bed pillows work great.

A sofa

Need a place to put that old cat-clawed sofa that's gathering dust in the garage? Bring it to school and create your own writing living room. Be prepared. Everyone will want to sit on it, so you may need a sign-up sheet for your students.

Writing carpet squares

This works especially well if you don't have carpeting in your room. Hand students a 2' x 2' carpet square and they can create an office anywhere in the room.

Beanbag chairs

A few beanbag chairs are all it takes to create an instant literacy living room in your class. Though students will have to take turns, they will appreciate the lounging atmosphere these chairs create.

Do We Have Control Issues?

I once presented an in-service workshop at a Catholic high school in Connecticut. After the workshop, a nun came into the classroom as I was packing up my materials. She was just over four feet tall and wore a traditional black habit. When I looked up, I saw the strangest sight. She was moving around the room, lining up the feet of each desk so that they stood exactly where the tiles met at right angles. I observed her for a while and then politely asked what she was doing. She looked back up at me over her shoulder with a nervous, almost embarrassed smile on her face. "Things get a little crazy if I don't do this," she said.

I remember thinking to myself, *Do we have control issues here?* But when you think about it, isn't there a little bit of that little nun in all of us? The physical design of a room says a lot about who you are as a teacher. How much control are you willing to give up? How much do you retain? Let's take a minute and rethink the space in your room.

Alter Your Feng Shui

In a traditional classroom, the teacher sat at the front of the room and the students sat in rows. Information flowed from the teacher to the student like in this diagram on the left.

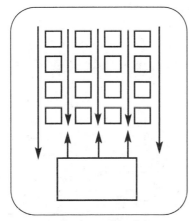

Energy flow in a traditional classroom

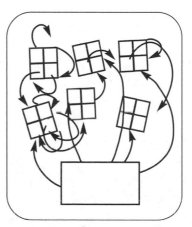

New energy flow

In a writing classroom the information flow is more decentralized. Teachers don't read every draft of every paper a student writes. Students write as much for one another and the larger world as they do for the teacher or the assignments. Teachers encourage this pattern. In such a classroom, the information flow might look more like the diagram on the right (previous page).

In this flow pattern, the teacher is still a central figure, but the information does not flow in a linear pattern back and forth as though there were no other students in the room. Groups of students, the class as a whole, and the outside world all serve the role of an audience that previously was filled by a single teacher. This dynamic team model is closer to the way most companies in the world function today than is the old way of teaching.

Preparing Your Students for the 21st Century

Years ago, I met a young man on a plane who had just graduated from college and landed a job at Motorola. He was a member of a team of 250 people designing a chip that would parallel-park a car automatically. I asked him if they also made a chip that would complain about your parking skills like a backseat driver. Ha, ha. Then I asked him what it is like to work on a team that large. In my entire experience in school, I only worked with one other person, Julianna Hill, in Miss Foley's fourth-grade class. We collaborated on a project on agriculture, and she insisted on reading it to the class by herself. (I'm still mad about that.)

The young man paused for a moment and said, "Well, I work for a half hour at my desk, then I get stuck. Then I have to go find someone else on the team who knows more than me." He paused again and said, "Do you know what the big problem is at Motorola?" I said, "No."

"The people who know the most have their office doors closed. They are the upper management—the men over 50 who don't always have time to deal with younger members of the team."

It struck me that those guys with their doors closed probably had the same schooling experience I had—desks in rows, teachers at the front who graded and passed back their work. The top-down information flow cripples companies in today's global economy.

When you move the furniture to create a more decentralized, real writing classroom, you are preparing students for success in the 21st century.

A FLOOR PLAN FOR WRITING

For a minute, forget about the classroom that you teach in and all the desks and chairs and tables. Imagine creating your own floor plan. Here are some questions to consider.

- Where is my desk?
- Where is the share area?
- Is there a full-group share area?
- Where can students meet to confer with one another?
- Where will I confer with students?
- When conducting a lesson, where will I stand or sit?

Empty Box

Now that you have created your ideal floor plan, take a look at your real classroom and see how much of your ideal you can squeeze into it. Remember, anything that's not bolted to the floor is fair game to move or remove. You are the CEO of your classroom, and the best CEOs always turn to their workers for the best ideas on how to improve a company. Have your students design their own ideal classrooms and see what great ideas you get from them.

Debriefing

How far is your classroom from your ideal design? How can you bridge the gap? What can you purchase or find to make your classroom friendlier to writing? If you were locked overnight in your classroom, would you feel like you were living in an institution? Or would there be cozy nooks to work and relax in?

CHOICE: THE FINAL INGREDIENT

While they are both critical ingredients, time and space on their own won't get you a real writing classroom. In fact, you can create a writing classroom without much time and space, as long as you have a healthy dose of the final ingredient: *choice*.

Consider the classroom where the teacher writes a writing assignment or writing prompt on the board. The students have no choice but to write about what the teacher has asked them to write about. The teacher may be a wonderful teacher, and indeed, I have had many wonderful teachers who taught like this, but if that wonderful teacher wants to turn his students into wonderful writers, the next logical step is for him to say, "I've just written an idea of something to write about on the board. Does anyone else have ideas of something to write about?" Then this teacher might write some of the students' ideas on his blackboard.

The next level of giving up choice might be that the students have their own writer's notebooks. The blackboard is now only an accessory on which the teacher might model a mini-lesson and give students ideas to fuel their own writing-idea generators. There are many ways for a teacher to hand off choice to students and still maintain a comfort zone of authority over the class. Teachers must decide for themselves what method best fits their teaching style.

Great works of western literature that began as writing prompts

The First Day of Writing Class

Let's imagine it's the first day of school and it is writing time. You have just told your students that they can write about anything they want to write about. A dull haze settles over the room. Eyes turn glassy and the first barely audible whines begin to emerge. "I don't know what to write about." Stop! This is the moment at which some teachers give up teaching real writing and break down and put an idea of their own up on the board.

Let's replay the scene, only this time you are the student and not the teacher. It's the first day of school and I have just told you that you can write about whatever you want to write about. A dull haze settles over you. A voice inside your head whines, "I don't know what to write about." You say it to me, and I say, "Fantastic! That's where all writers begin. Writers don't always know what they want to write about in the beginning. That takes time, thought, and writing itself. We need blank moments, duhhhh moments. Moments to think. You are on the right track. I am so proud of you. I am so glad you didn't just pretend to write something because you thought I wanted you to."

How do you feel now? Maybe you are still feeling clueless, but I have told you it's okay to feel that way. In fact, it's more than okay, it is an essential part of the process. I call this "pimple time," time to sit staring at the paper as you grow a big pimple on your forehead.

TRY THIS!

WRITE ABOUT HOW YOU CAN'T WRITE

X Real choice writing must always include pimple time. You can also call it staring. I call it free staring and it is part of my writing process. In his book of essays, *Expect the Unexpected*, Donald Murray describes his shock when he observed a classroom where all the students wrote on command and not one sat there staring into space. How could real writing be happening with no time for contemplation?

Here's an effective assignment that helps with fluency. Quick-write for seven minutes about how you can't think of what to write about.

Debriefing

Was it easy to write about not writing? What did you learn about writing by writing about not knowing what to write about? Did you eventually find something to write about?

> I am sitting in Ms. English's fourth grade class trying to write a paragraph using spaced caper words. My mind is blank like piece of white paper. I see myself in the middle of my class with Branden on my right and a wall on my left. The students in front of me, behind me, and to the right of me are all writing their paragraphs. I am still looking at a blank piece of paper with a blank mind. I look at the clock, and the hands are moving fast. Time is running out for me. Everyone has finished their paragraphs but me. My mind was still blank like my paper. The bell rang and I went to my grandmother's portable to finish my writing assignment. I needed an idea. I finally decided to write about having to write this with no ideas.

Example of a quick-write by a fourth grader

PEOPLE, PLACES, EVENTS

Another way to fill the void of pimple time is to have students make lists of people, places, and things to write about. The celebrated author Henry Miller didn't start writing until he was past the age of 40. One night he began making lists of all the people he had known, places he had been, and events that he remembered. By the end of the night he had enough ideas for three books. Here's your chance to try out Miller's strategy. Draw three vertical lines down one of your notebook pages to make columns. In the left column, write the heading "People." Write "Places" atop the middle column and "Events" on top of the right column. Pay special attention to how the memory of a place helps you to remember the people you met there, and how remembering a person can make a place or event emerge in your mind. Let your list grow for pages.

#1 ✱
Ideas
—
3 columns

Debriefing

Was it easy to make your list? Did you find yourself remembering more as you brainstormed? When you go back through your list, are there any events you really want to write about?

Another way to help students find ideas to write about is to help them locate their center of authority. None of us really understands the things we are good at until we take the time to make a list.

#2
Center of authority
Lists
a.

WHAT ARE YOU GOOD AT? AUTHORITY LISTS

What are you good at? At first, you may say "nothing." But think for a minute, and you may find some ideas. Take a look at my list.

I'm good at . . .

- staying in bed for the longest possible time after the alarm goes off
- waiting in line patiently
- being nice to telemarketers
- writing

- thinking up cartoons
- talking to people on planes
- running

Make your own "I'm good at" list. Next, make your own "I'm not good at" list. Here's mine.

b.

I'm not good at . . .

- handwriting
- dancing
- swimming
- lying

Debriefing

Which list was easier to make? Did making the lists help you to remember people, places, or events? If so, try writing down some of them.

Another way to find writing ideas from real life is to make a timeline of your days on Earth.

#3 timeline of your life so far

TRY THIS!

A TIMELINE OF YOUR LIFE *key moments.*

Talk to your students about key moments in your life. The psychologist Abraham Maslow called these moments that changed us in some way "peak experiences." Birth might be called our first peak experience. What happened in your life that you would describe as a peak experience?

You can create your own unique timeline in your notebook.

Born————————————————————————Now

Debriefing

What was it like to make your timeline? What experiences jumped out at you? What experiences would you consider writing about?

The Long Walk to Freedom

In 1998, I traveled from St. Louis, Missouri, to Capetown, South Africa, with eight teachers. We conducted in-service workshops in writing for teachers from the poorest neighborhoods of Guguletu, a sprawling ghetto on the outskirts of Capetown. I had gone with the Amy Biehl Foundation, a nonprofit relief agency run by the parents of Amy Biehl, a Stanford graduate who had been murdered in a senseless race riot in 1994, which was just months before the first free elections in South Africa. Amy Biehl's parents became national celebrities in South Africa when they came to the country after her murder and asked the question, "Why did this

Me with friends in Nelson Mandela's cell

happen?" Their pursuit of an answer to this question led them to create a foundation to continue the work Amy had started in seventh grade, when she first heard about Nelson Mandela's imprisonment. The story made national news in the United States, and several times the Biehls appeared on *60 Minutes*, once with the murderer of their daughter, who is now a leader in the organization.

I didn't know it before I left, but going on this trip was going to be a peak experience for me. At left is me standing in Nelson Mandela's prison cell on Robben Island with Joyce Foster and Gloria Sadler, two teachers from St. Louis.

This cell is where Mandela wrote his autobiography, *Long Walk to Freedom*, on scraps of toilet paper and whatever else he could find. On the next page (bottom photo) is Ahmed Kathrada, who gave us a tour of the prison. He stands next to the picture of himself when he was a young man, the day he was arrested with Mandela and the other seven men, who were called the Rivonia 8.

Kathrada had the cell across from Mandela's. He was an excellent editor so Mandela would give him his writing to correct. Kathrada then sent it to a man in another cell block who would copy it in extremely small print on eggshell paper. The pages were then bound into a notebook folder and smuggled to Switzerland. An entire writing workshop took place in that prison even though prisoners were not allowed to talk with one another. One popular method of conferring was to write on crumpled paper napkins and leave them on the cafeteria trays. The dishwasher became the mailman later when he took the crumpled napkins out of his pocket and delivered them to addressees.

Seeing how a few prisoners were able to create an entire secret civilized society within an uncivilized prison gave me a strange sense of hope for the public school system. Perhaps the creativity and ingenuity of individual teachers and administrators could overcome the dehumanizing impulse to standardize and reduce children and learning to numbers.

Me with Zunade Dharsey

Here I am standing on Robben Island with Zunade Dharsey, one of the new friends I made on this trip.

I call this photo "Batman and Robin on Robben Island." We are standing in the spot where Nelson Mandela gathered seaweed, one of the many jobs the prisoners were forced to do. Zunade spent most of his formative years hurling stones at policeman and being arrested for political activities. He was a brilliant man, and he knew how to tell a story. At one point I asked him why he had never written his stories down. He turned to me with an almost frightened look on his face and said, "I am afraid that if I write them down, they will no longer be mine; someone else will own them. You can write my stories, Barry. Put them in a book if you want. I won't care. I promise."

I am finally doing what he told me to do. Here is one of Zunade's stories.

Mandela compatriot Ahmed Kathrada

> In the South African prisons, the political prisoners made the rules and the other prisoners, usually common criminals, followed them. One rule involved food. By order of the government, men with darker skin received less food than men with lighter skin. The rule Zunade made was that all prisoners pool their food and divide it evenly. And if it was your birthday, you got a special treat. Every meal had a dessert of stale bread pudding with a spoonful of sugar on top that often melted into a puddle. All prisoners poured their puddle of sugar onto the birthday boy's cake and everyone sang "Happy Birthday." Even this dark, smelly, horrible prison could not kill the spirit of joy and celebration among the prisoners.

When Zunade told this story, I could tell he was proud of the rule he had made. He was smiling.

Just a few months after we returned from South Africa, we got some sad news. Zunade Dharsey had died in a tragic accident. He had tried to save the life of a total stranger who was caught in a riptide at the beach. As I heard the news, all I could think about was how glad I was that we got to know him and his stories. Life can be so fragile, so fleeting, and we are here for such a short time. When we die, all we leave is our stories. Though your students' stories may not be as dramatic as Zunade's, remember the spirit of Zunade Dharsey as you create a classroom where children tell their real stories.

Think of your class as the Long Walk to Freedom of Expression. Don't be discouraged by problems from within or outside. Like all long walks, take it one step at a time.

In the next chapter, we are going to learn how to create a question culture in your class to fuel writing in any subject.

"YEAH, BUT . . ."
Readers' Questions Answered

You must be kidding. If I let kids write about what they want to write about, it might take them half an hour to figure out what to write about. I can't spare this precious time. Do you have any idea how jam-packed our day is?

I do. It really is hard to find time to write, and I guarantee you will feel anxious watching as your students sit there twiddling their thumbs, thinking about what to write about. But if you stick to this regular time you will find it gets easier and easier for your students to identify topics they feel passionate about and want to explore in writing. A regular time allows them to think about their writing earlier in the day or the day before. You can ask them to write down their writing goals for the day in the morning as well. A writing workshop is like an engine for writing that drives all the writing a child does each day. Your writing workshop is not just a language arts block. Incorporate social studies writing and science writing with this time once a week. Find a way to overlap other subjects into writing time if that's what it takes to get the necessary writing time for your students.

We only have 30 minutes for writing.

This is one I hear a lot. Certain writing programs devote only 30 minutes a day to free writing time, and within this time they sometimes include a mini-lesson. The last time I was asked this question was in an auditorium with 200 elementary school teachers. I asked them to close their eyes, and then I asked them to raise their hands if they regularly went over the 30-minute writing time. Most of the teachers raised their hands. I told them it appeared to me that they did not have only 30 minutes for writing, and suggested that they take control of their curriculum to make it work for them. "You are the professionals," I told them. "It's your job to teach, not to follow a prefab program." If the program is any good you will be able to adapt it to the needs of your students. I have been to schools where creative teachers have taken the most structured reading and writing programs and adapted them to their own needs. If your administrator questions you about this, tell him, "If you allow me to teach in a way that engages them in real learning, the results will speak for themselves."

Yeah, but my district purchased a program and they expect me to use it. What do I do? Quit?

A program does not replace a teacher. If that's what the district truly thinks, then you already have lost your job. Only the most narrow-thinking, bureaucratic administrator would insist that a teacher follow a writing program on a day-by-day basis. I have seen this happen and the results are not pretty. Whenever the programs fail, these administrators tend to blame the teachers anyway for not following them closely enough. So, it's a kind of cycle of failure that encourages districts to buy more programs and to discount the work that teachers do. The only way to break this cycle is to insist on controlling your own teaching destiny. Don't get me wrong—you may really like the program and want to follow it exactly. That is fine as long as it is your decision. But you are free to deviate from the program if it makes no sense to you or your students, or add your creative touch to its lessons. I know of very few teachers who have been fired for following their own creative instincts. Usually they end up being hailed as gifted teachers whose students excel.

Where do writing and reading programs come from and why are they so dominant in American education?

As a boy, I traveled with my parents to Sturbridge Village in Massachusetts, a living museum of American life in 1840, when the first public schools were appearing. The schoolhouse was built by the community so the children would have a place to read and write. There were no teachers, only a farmer, whom the community subsidized for a few months of the year to run the school. Since the farmer had no training as a teacher, he needed a book to help him. Enter the basal reader and the writing primer, ancestors of the modern reading and writing programs.

Eventually, communities learned that a real teacher could do much more than just a farmer and a basal. Farmers tended their crops and professional teachers were hired to run the schools. These well-educated teachers, usually women, could create their own lessons if the village could not afford schoolbooks. From the start, reading and writing programs were in a subtle competition with teachers. This competition continues today in American public schools, only now the stakes are much higher. Billions of dollars ride on textbook adoptions, and creative teachers who make their own lessons are seen as obstacles to profit. Though teachers are often asked to vote on which textbook to adopt, they are rarely offered the "none of the above" choice by their district.

For a comprehensive history of reading programs in America, I recommend reading Patrick Shannon's book *Reading Against Democracy: The Broken Promises of Reading Instruction.*

Don't kids start acting up when they have an hour to write? How do I avoid this?

This may be a problem at first, especially when students are not used to having a sustained writing time and if they are used to being told exactly what to write about. You will find yourself responding to "But I don't know what to write about" over and over again. Here are some simple suggestions to help these students before they get too frustrated and start acting out.

1. Use background music to create an atmosphere for writing and soothe savage writing beasts. I like Celtic harp music that tinkles in the background.

2. Model your own sense of frustration before they face it. Example, "I am so stumped, I really don't know what to write about today. What should I do?" You may find that your best suggestions come from writers who face the same struggles.

3. Make sure your students know that writing time can be thinking time. Making lists of ideas, scribbling memories and stray thoughts, or just sitting there thinking is writing. The pressure to produce words on paper sometimes short-circuits a student's ability to realize what writing time can be.

4. Healthy snacks can help a writer to think and a class to feel that something special is happening. Writing time should be an oasis of thought and reflection in the institutional desert that is sometimes school. Food relaxes and refreshes.

I teach kindergarten and first grade. What if all they do is draw?

Talking is the first language mode we learn. Drawing is the second. Writing is the third. I have heard a kindergartner explain her picture for half an hour, even when she has only drawn a little squiggle on a page ("This line is my brother going into the house and then he comes out of the house with a sandwich.") As a teacher you are helping your students cross the bridge from drawing to writing. Start by labeling some of the things they draw and encourage them to do the same, sounding out the letters of the alphabet. One of my favorite idea-gathering activities for kindergartners is something I call "feeling trees." We start by talking about feelings and I list them on the board. Then I ask for a volunteer to come up and I trace the child's arm and hand. It looks like a tree and I call it a feeling tree. We write down a feeling in the center, and for each finger, we come up with a time we have felt that feeling, or an object, or a food, or a person who gives us that feeling. It's a great way to convert drawing into writing, and it shows students that in writing you can start with feelings as well as events. Drawing is also an important component of literacy in the graphically rich world we live in. To learn the ABCs of graphics for kids, I highly recommend the book *I See What You Mean* by Steve Moline. (Hey, that rhymes!)

I have 100-plus students. If they write every day, I have to read a lot of papers every night. How do I find time to do all that reading and still do all my other teacher preparation?

In a writing workshop, you don't have to read and comment extensively on every draft your student writes. Choose to look at early drafts and late drafts. Ask your students to include a letter explaining how a piece has evolved. If your students keep journals or notebooks, there is no need to comment extensively in order to see that they are doing the work. You are their teacher, but you are also a kind overseer or foreman who is making sure they are doing the work and encouraging them to keep going. Some of your reading will be in this vein. You also must take advantage of your students' abilities to assess and reflect on their own learning. *Seeking Diversity* by Linda Rief is an excellent resource for middle school and high school teachers interested in developing these qualities in their students.

CHAPTER 3

CREATING A QUESTION CULTURE THROUGH WRITING

few years ago, I went to visit two elementary schools in the same district. School A was what I call a question school. School B was an answer school. When I visited the question school, the students and the teachers seemed engaged in learning. The desks were arranged in pods of four; students asked meaningful questions spontaneously, and seemed to have genuine interest in what I had to teach them about writing. There was a casual atmosphere, and the teachers seemed to be as excited about learning as they were about teaching.

> Writing is a lot easier if you have something to say.
>
> —*Sholem Asch*

The answer school was a different story. The children sat in rows with the teachers patrolling like wardens, peering over students' shoulders, as their young charges wrote very little and covered their papers when strangers approached. Some teachers even chose not to participate in my workshop, but sat at their desks, correcting stacks of worksheets. Special-education students in these classrooms had their own separate islands, surrounded by aides. There was a palpable feeling of boredom in the air. It reminded me of my own school years, when the high point of the day was inhaling a few whiffs of the new purple mimeo worksheet.

I decided to push the envelope a bit and try something to change the culture of the answer school. I asked the students to think of a topic that intrigued them and to make a list of 10 curious questions about that topic. Like the first caveman who brought fire to the tribe, I would bring the light of questioning to the answer tribe who lived in cold and boring darkness. They seemed to take to the task well. Their heads perked up; their pencils scribed along. In ten minutes they each had a topic of interest and a list of questions. I called on the first student, and he stood up to share.

"My topic is hockey," he said proudly, "and here are my questions."

"Do you play hockey with a puck?"

"Do you play hockey with a stick?"

"Do you play hockey with a . . ."

"Okay," I said, cringing a bit with that sinking feeling in my gut. This lesson might not be working. "Next." Another boy stood up.

"My topic is baseball and here are my questions,"

"Do you play baseball with a bat?"

"Do you play baseball with a ball?"

"Great," I said. The charade was over. You have two choices when a lesson is going down in flames:

1. You wait for the bell.

2. You get real.

When you choose the first option, nobody learns anything, but things keep moving. But if you are brave enough to choose the second option, miracles can happen because you have dared to allow a genuine, messy, dumb, clueless moment into your tidy classroom. And when you admit the feelings of helpless ignorance brought on by a failed lesson, you are no longer the "velveteen teacher." You are real.

It was a good day. I chose the second option. I asked these kids what a question was, and it was clear that they knew. It was clear they were curious. They knew how to think. The only problem was, they didn't see school as a place where thinking should occur. They were trained to see school as a place to give answers, not a place to raise questions. You can create a question culture in an answer school, but it takes time. You can't do it one lesson, as I tried to.

Writing can be the single best tool for forging a question culture in your school and your classroom; indeed, it can help make learning real. In this chapter, we will explore things any teacher of any subject or any grade level can do to create a question culture with writing.

AN OUT-OF-THIS-WORLD STORY

A Lesson From Hawaii

This is Ellison Onizuka, the first Hawaiian astronaut. He was a hero to the children of the islands of Hawaii, and although he died in the space shuttle *Challenger* in 1986, his stories live on, like those of all great teachers. Back in the 1970s, my friend Joyce Kohfeldt traveled with Ellison Onizuka to present to assemblies in many Hawaiian schools. Before one such trip, there was a nervous phone call from the school's principal. "Don't worry, Mr. Onizuka. We are not going to let the children ask questions," he said. "We have scripted the questions so you won't be embarrassed." Ellison Onizuka replied, "I will not visit your school if you do not let the children ask any question they want as I stand before them." The principal conceded, and Ellison Onizuka went to the school.

Ellison Onizuka

Now just for a moment, imagine Ellison Onizuka, the first native Hawaiian astronaut, standing in front of a gymnasium filled with young children. He has just asked them if they have any questions. What do you think the first question was that they asked him? You guessed it. "How do you go to the bathroom on the space shuttle?"

Ellison Onizuka did not even blink. He launched with great gusto into a description of the $23 million toilet with the vacuum-seal seat on the *Columbia* space shuttle. He even went as far as describing some of the more disgusting ways *Apollo* astronauts removed their waste, methods involving spatulas and stainless steel canisters. Next question. He called on a little girl up front, who couldn't have been more than a second grader. She had been waving her hand wildly.

"What's one thing you did on the space shuttle that you never told anyone about?"

Ellison Onizuka paused for a minute as though deep in contemplation, and then turned to that principal who seemed to have "I told you so" written all over his face, and said, forthrightly, "Find me a VCR, please."

The principal returned a few minutes later with a wobbly media cart with a TV and VCR. The astronaut popped in a VHS tape and an image appeared on-screen. There was Ellison Onizuka, floating in zero gravity, opening a bag of Skittles and dumping them out. As the brightly colored candies floated around the spaceship, Ellison Onizuka snapped at them like a wild puppy dog chomping at butterflies.

What I love about this story is that you don't get the joyful answer to that wonderful second question without the first bathroom question. The act of asking questions and answering questions is an organic process, not an arbitrary task. And like farming, it starts with tilling the soil and adding at least some type of fertilizer. But how do we begin the tilling, especially if we teach in a school where the field is as hard and barren as a Wal-Mart parking lot?

The first thing to note about a question culture is that some questions are far more interesting than others.

> **LANE'S SIXTH LAW OF LITERACY**
>
> All questions are not created equal.

Note: In an answer culture, all questions are equal; they come numbered at the end of chapters, and you have to answer all of them or points will be deducted from your final grade. How do we start creating a question culture?

TRY THIS!

INTERROGATIVE CPR: PUTTING THE QUEST BACK IN QUESTION

Here is a lesson that appears in my forthcoming book, *Non-fiction Writers/Readers Toolbox*. It is my all-time favorite way to teach students the true value of questions to a writer.

Model It

Talk with your students about boring topics. Make a list on the bored. I mean *board*. Here are some that come to mind.

- Socks
- Laundry
- Folding laundry
- Insurance
- Millard Fillmore
- Fractions
- Algebra

Now, pick one from the list and ask your students to ask you questions about it. Tell students that they can ask different types of questions.

- *Historical question:* Who created the first insurance company?
- *Obvious:* What is insurance?
- *Mathematical:* How much profit does the average insurance company make in a year?

Do It

Now, have your students pick their own boring topic. Set the timer for five minutes and have them brainstorm as many questions as they can in this time to breathe life into that topic. If you teach social studies, science, or math, you might want to choose boring subjects in your own area of study.

Debriefing

Did your topic get more interesting the more you asked questions? Do some questions want to be answered more than others? What is the difference between an interesting question and a not so interesting question?

From Infinity and Beyond

In Carl Sagan's novel *Contact*, the protagonist, Ellie, a physicist, recalls her first moment of wonder about the universe. It was in a high school algebra class, and she had encountered the concept of infinity with the mathematical concept of pi. She asked the teacher if there was any way to calculate infinity, and he bluntly told her not to waste her time on such a dumb question. There were some things that mathematicians just had to accept as givens. Only years later, in graduate school, while studying for her Ph.D., did she find out her question was not dumb at all. Every great civilization in the history of humanity had struggled with this question. Furthermore, the concept of pi was a compromise that not even all great mathematicians accepted. In other words, they were still trying to answer the dumb question she had asked in high school. Her teacher had been teaching and thinking like a math textbook. It was Ellie who had been thinking like a mathematician. She knew that all questions are not created equal. Some are far more fascinating than others.

LANE'S SEVENTH LAW OF LITERACY

The only "dumb" questions are the ones you don't want to know the answers to.

Here's another way to teach students to value some questions more than others.

TRY THIS!

THE QUESTION BLITZ

Model It

Talk to your students about the importance of real curiosity and passion when addressing a writing subject, whether it's a personal essay, a research project, or a work of fiction. A question is the engine of writing. Rev it up and your vehicle is going to move forward fast.

Next, give an example of a topic you want to write about, and ask students to ask you questions. Write their questions on the board. Remind them of the various types of questions they can ask from the last lesson and encourage them to create their own categories or just be curious.

Now look at all the questions they asked you and ask them which three are the most intriguing. Which three do they really want to know the answer to? Discuss how those are the three questions you are going to strive to answer with help from a library or Internet research.

Do It

Ask students to spend 15 minutes writing down as many questions as they can about their topic.

Ask students to pick the three most intriguing questions and put them at the top of a blank piece of paper with a line under them and plenty of space for more to be written. (Note: For the most dramatic effect have students write their questions with markers on big pieces of chart paper.)

Next, either hang their questions around the room or pass them around. Have students put a checkmark next to their most intriguing question and add more questions at the bottom of the page.

When the students get back their original papers, they note the checkmarks made by the class and read all the new questions.

Now, tell students to pick their favorite three questions, write them on another sheet of paper, and head off to do research at the library or on the Internet.

Debriefing

Was it easy to pick the most interesting questions? What is the difference between an interesting question and a not so interesting question? Did the class pick the same question you would have picked as the most interesting? Did you find some of the class's questions more interesting than yours?

The Dump Truck, Google Truck Essay

When I was in school, we wrote dump truck essays, or reports. We'd go to the library, find some dusty *Encyclopedia Britannica*, and copy out some entries, spelling a few words wrong so the teacher would think we had written it. It seemed like a skill back then. Today, the Google truck will come right to your desk and dump this type of information in your lap at light speed. In the age of information, getting information is no longer a problem. It is how we organize, think through, and package that information that becomes the real skill. In the last exercise,

students began to see that getting curious and choosing some questions over others begins this process. They traded in their dump truck for a laser beam guided by those questions. Now it's time to experience this same process through public speaking.

TRY THIS!

HOLD YOUR OWN PRESS CONFERENCE

A live television press conference is one sure sign of a constitutional democracy. As a president or other public leader fields questions from a hungry press corps, there is often pressure to be more candid and spontaneous than he wants to be. In a failing democracy, press conferences are simply look-good media events. The questions are scripted so as not to embarrass the leader, and asked politely one at a time. The reporters are handpicked to ask certain questions so the leader can prepare his responses beforehand. The leader refuses to answer or stonewalls any follow-up questions and instead calls on the next reporter, whom he knows is going to ask the question with the prepared answer. A phony press conference is as sad and boring as a scripted lesson from a textbook. Let's make learning and democracy real for our students by showing them what a real press conference looks like.

Model It

1. Bring in a tape of a press conference. The best ones can be found on C-SPAN at any hour of the day. Discuss with students what a press conference is. What makes a press conference interesting?

2. Tell your students about one of your hobbies or a special interest you have. Tell them they are the press corps and must ask you questions to find what interests them about the topic. If you have done the Try This on page 49, remind them of how we can bring to life any subject with interesting questions.

3. Ask a student to record the questions students come up with, or do it yourself. Whenever a student asks a question for which you don't know the answer, say, "That's a good question" and put a star next to it.

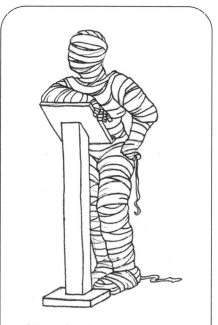

"No Madam, being a mummy was not my first career choice."

4. After students have done some research on a topic, have them stand in front of the class for a brief press conference. Write down all the questions on a piece of paper and hand it to the writer when the press conference is over.

5. Ask students to pick some favorite questions and research them.

6. After doing more research, students can do another press conference, only this time you get to become the subject they researched.

Debriefing

What was it like to do your press conference? Did you feel like an expert on your subject or did you feel you needed to do more research? Did the questions get you thinking about your subject in a different way? What new questions do you want to know the answers to?

LOBSTER NEUROLOGY

On a short flight from Pittsburgh to St. Louis, I met a lobster neurologist. I kid you not. This was a grown man, a full professor from Cornell University who had spent his entire formative life studying the brains of lobsters. What a rare opportunity, I thought to myself. He settled in next to me on the aisle seat, slipping his duct-taped briefcase (my kind of man) under the seat in front of him. I began asking him questions about lobsters, and on that short flight, I became an expert on lobster brains.

Here are just a few intriguing facts I learned:

- Lobsters mate for life.
- The female always chooses the mate in lobster land.
- Unlike some human beings, the female is extremely particular about whom she chooses.
- Lobster men have to dance or they won't get a mate.
- Lobsters can live as long as 120 years, and some reach a size of six feet long.
- Lobsters are arachnids, the same species as spiders.
- Lobsters turn red when you boil them.
- The most humane way to kill a lobster is to freeze it.

At one point in our conversation, I asked the question most New Englanders with years of stored-up lobster guilt have to ask: Do lobsters feel pain? He paused a moment and then launched into a short lecture on the evolution of the human brain and the lobster brain. The human brain weighs two and a half pounds and contains several billion brain cells. The lobster brain weighs only a few ounces and contains only 20,000 brain cells. Most of the human brain is devoted to pain. We have the primitive brain that feels pain directly, and the cerebral cortex which feels pain and pretends not to (highly developed in teachers, no doubt). Lobsters do feel pain, but not the acute pain we associate with human pain. There are simply not enough nerves there. A lobster's pain is more like a general malaise.

When I tell this story to students or teachers, I ask them which facts are the most intriguing. Which made them go "ooh!" inside? I call these the "ooh!" facts, and all real fiction and nonfiction writers know about them. An "ooh!" fact in an essay or research report can be that bit of information that changes how you see, well, a lobster, for example. In a fictional narrative it can be that information about a character or a plot point that draws you in.

"Yes, indeed, we did have many young, but my wife and I ate them. The rest went to college."

LANE'S EIGHTH LAW OF LITERACY

All facts are not created equal.
Some are much more interesting than others.

TRY THIS!

TEACH "OOH!" FACTS

Writers make choices all the time. There is just too much to write about, and besides, not everything is that interesting. Some facts stand out from the pack. Like hounds on a scent, nonfiction writers root out the "ooh!" facts and build their writing around them.

Model It

Not all facts are created equal. Some are more interesting than others. Tell this to your students and then prove it. Go to a Web site like www.hookedonfacts.com

or just type an interesting fact into a search engine and see how many Web sites pop up. Next, pull the most interesting facts and mix them with very general facts. For example:

- Lobsters live in the ocean.
- Lobsters are eaten at seafood restaurants.
- A lobster can live to be 120 years old.

Which is the "ooh!" fact?

Do It

Ask your students to find "ooh!" facts about any topic.
1. Here are a few Web sites to visit:

- www.hookedonfacts.com
- www.interestingfact.com
- www.nicefacts.com
- www.amusingfacts.com

2. Find as many interesting facts as you can in 20 minutes.

3. Share your facts.

Debriefing

What makes your facts interesting? Did any facts make the class go "ooh!"? What new questions grow from your "ooh!" facts?

Now that you know about "ooh!" facts, here is a way to understand how to use them in the context of a lesson.

TRY THIS!
START WITH A SPARK

When a piece of writing focuses on a writer's genuine interest in a subject, great things happen; yet many writers continue to write in boring and predictable ways. These mini-lessons teach students to break the mold, and find the passion in their subject.

Model It

1. Go to the library and find several biographies of one person, like Mahatma Gandhi or Nelson Mandela or George Washington. Make sure some start in typical boring fashion. There is usually no problem finding these, but if you can't, make up some of your own, e.g., "George Washington was the first president of the United States. He is known as the father of our country."

2. Talk to your students about the importance of beginning a piece of writing with passion. You don't get a fire if you don't have a spark to start with. Read the leads to a few of the biographies and ask the students to tell you which are the "sparky" ones.

Do It

Now we get to learn this lesson through our own research and writing. Ask your students, "If you were to write a biography of someone sitting in this room, what would be the most boring and predictable way of beginning it?" 'He was born. . . .' You have seven minutes to interview a partner in this room, and then I am going to call 'switch' and your partner will have seven minutes to interview you. In the last seven minutes, you are going to write the lead to your partner's biography, putting the most interesting thing you found into that lead." Share the leads with one another and with the class.

Reinforce the concept for finding the "ooh!" fact by rereading some of the more interesting leads you have found. Remind students more than once that you are not looking for a lead that is a list of facts about that person. You want them to pick one interesting fact and build their lead around it.

Debriefing

Was it hard to find "ooh!" facts about the person you interviewed? What did it feel like to be interviewed? When you began to write your lead, what process did you go through to find the best place to start? If you wrote more than one lead, what is the difference between the two?

TOWARD A UNIFIED FIELD THEORY OF WRITING

Albert Einstein spent the last years of his life trying to find a unified field theory of physics, a theory that would connect all the disparate phenomena physicists had struggled with for centuries. He failed, but before his death I met him at the hairdresser, and discussed with him my unified field theory for writing. By the way, in case you didn't know, Einstein put a lot of product in his hair.

Me with the (waxy) Albert Einstein

Before I divulge my theory, let me say that this is the part of the book where I may alienate some high school English teachers and most of the writing textbook publishers who created the books we used when I was in school. These books and teachers purported that there were many different forms of writing: expository, persuasive, fiction, essays, how-tos, you name it. Not only that, there were also different types of paragraphs and sentences. A student had to master these minute forms before daring to call himself or herself a writer. The books would have sections on descriptive writing or persuasive writing, and there would be even more differentiation between types of writing. Students would be asked to memorize and recite rhetorical styles, support each topic sentence with three supporting details, and on and on.

These activities may have had some value for students wanting good grades in AP English classes, but they have little to do with real writing. In his groundbreaking book, *The School Essay Manifesto*, writing researcher Thomas Newkirk says, "We must reclaim the essay from the textbooks where it has been imprisoned." Throughout the small book, Newkirk shows how what is known as the school essay is an invention of 1950s English composition textbooks. Great essays, according to Newkirk, track the movement of the human mind.

> **LANE'S NINTH LAW OF LITERACY**
>
> Great writing is not a product of great formulas.
> Great writing tracks the movement of a single human mind.

This law leads directly to my unified field theory of writing.

> **LANE'S FIRST UNIFIED FIELD THEORY OF WRITING**
>
> All writing, no matter what form or genre, is essentially the same.
> The only difference lies in the source or information.

In nonfiction writing the source might be found in the library or on the Internet or maybe a live interview (as in the press conference mini-lesson). In narrative writing, the source might be your own memory or, in the case of fiction, your imagination. In what is sometimes called transactional writing or analytical writing, the source might be the writer's brain and its ability to make connections between text, life, and other sources. The sources of information and ideas change, but the basic process of writing is maintained.

In this chapter, we have seen the power of curiosity as an important factor in this process. Once you make the commitment to create a question culture with your students, amazing things can happen. But how do you sustain this culture throughout the school year and bring it to all the subjects you teach? How do you bring a suppleness of mind to your students' writings and not fall into the trap of just doing assignments?

In the next chapter we explore how to create and sustain a playground of possibility in your students' writing.

"YEAH, BUT . . ."

Readers' Questions Answered

My school has an answer culture and wants me to follow a program for teaching expository writing. Students are required to support topic sentences with three details. You know the drill. How can I justify teaching in this way?

The Lone Paragraph Arranger

I don't believe it hurts kids to learn these simple formulas; the key is not to present this formula as the only way to write. The trouble with most programs is that they do present it this way. As a result, they get limited results and, within a year, all students' writing sounds the same and all students groan when it's time to write. I recommend a book by Gretchen Bernabei called *Reviving the Essay: How to Teach Structure Without Formula*. It's an antidote to any one-dimensional writing program. As I describe later in Chapter 11, Bernabei's book shows students many structures that bring success to writers. She also describes how to find your own structure, something that all writers learn to do.

My kindergartners don't seem to understand what a question is. When I ask them for questions, they tell me stories.

Kindergartners ask great questions, but don't ask them to ask you a question, because they will tell a story. Instead, engage their curiosity by posing a question of your own and you will find they generate many questions. I teach kindergartners the difference between inside questions (feelings questions) and outside questions (thing questions). How big was the cat? *(outside question)* How did you feel when the cat chased you? *(inside question)*

My high school students have been taught how to write research papers with note cards. Do they have to unlearn note cards to learn a new way?

Note cards are still useful when learning how to structure a research essay, once you have found your focus through the questioning process described in this chapter. The goal is to find your spark of interest and then structure your paper around the spark. Your note cards can help you enormously once you have the spark. I recommend the freshman English textbook *The Curious Researcher* by Bruce Ballenger. Ballenger has written the only research writing textbook I know that puts the voice of the writer before the form of the paper. Though it is written for college students, I have used ideas from this book right down to first grade.

My curriculum tells me I have to teach different types of writing: persuasive, narrative, transactive. Don't different types of writing require different teaching strategies? How does a unified theory of writing help me teach?

Different types of writing might require slightly different rhetorical teaching strategies, but one thing stays the same: The students have to have something to say. Form follows function. Find ways to teach that incorporate authentic reasons to write and your students will learn this valuable lesson.

I work with English language learners. Asking questions is an advanced skill and sometimes requires more vocabulary than they possess. How do I create a question culture when there is so much pressure just to have students perform at the minimum level?

I can tell you that your ELLs will increase their vocabulary the more you can engage their curiosity. Again, "A strong horse will pull any cart." I once worked with a Cambodian boy who wrote the story of his life in the killing fields. He was searching for words in the dictionary to describe his experiences and he made sure he found those words. Human beings, no matter what their language skills, are hooked on meaning. Use it as the engine for learning.

CHAPTER 4

A PLAYGROUND OF POSSIBILITY

Using a Writer's Notebook

I was in a van driving to the airport when I met a woman who was a corporate trainer. She worked with Kevin Carroll, who wrote a book called *Rules of the Red Rubber Ball: Find and Sustain Your Life's Work.* The author had been abandoned by his father and mother. He had found salvation at the local playground with a red rubber ball. Carroll had gone on to become a highly paid motivator at Nike and eventually an inspirational national speaker. The woman I met in the airport van had just returned from a workshop on innovation for 11,000 executives in a Cleveland arena. Their

> Fill your paper with the breathings of your heart.
>
> —*William Wordsworth*

DEAR JAMES,
THIS WRITING LACKS COHESION AND ORGANIZATION. YOU CONTINUALLY SHIFT POINT OF VIEW AND MAKE IT DIFFICULT FOR THE READER TO FOLLOW. ALSO, WATCH YOUR PUNCTUATION THE LAST 40 PAGES OF THIS BOOK ARE ONE SENTENCE, WHAT WERE YOU THINKING!
C— MS. GRUNDY

goal in the workshop was to teach the executives to play, an essential skill for any company trying to compete in global markets. Indeed, it is the skill that American companies are good at and the skill other countries strive to imitate. The woman told me, with a great sense of pride, that they had just conducted the world's largest pillow fight.

I reflected on what I had done the day before. I had worked with teachers in the state of Georgia, where several large counties had cancelled recess for all schools until test scores increased. The irony in that moment was so thick you could not cut it with a chainsaw. We were eliminating recess for kids and spending millions to train CEOs to play. Houston, we have a problem.

The importance of play in writing is often understated in writing textbooks. It is called prewriting strategies, as though these are just activities you do to prepare for the real activity, writing. If this were really true, writers would spend 99 percent of their time getting ready to write. Every letter they've written, note taken, stray idea scribbled in a notebook wouldn't count as real writing. Like students in the schools where everything a writer puts to paper is assessed and graded for teacher approval, this writer would always be waiting for the next assignment. I have visited schools where the first response to a writing assignment is "How many sentences do you want us to write?" These are schools seriously lacking in the play quotient and, as a result, the writing is flat as a Nebraska ski slope, and lifeless.

> ### LANE'S SECOND UNIFIED FIELD THEORY OF WRITING
>
> In all writing $E = PQ^2$.

All energy in a piece of writing is equal to the play quotient of the writer squared. If a writer has no sense of play, the prose will be lifeless and anemic, as though anybody could have written it.

So how do we increase the play quotients of the writers in our classrooms? What practical steps can teachers of all subjects and grade levels take to build innovative play into the literacy curriculum? How can we create a question culture through play and vastly improve our students' writing? How can we help students expand this culture outside the classroom walls and into the real world?

CONFESSIONS OF A WRITER'S NOTEBOOK FLUNKY

First off, I have a confession to make. I am a writer's notebook flunky. For years, I have bought notebooks of all sizes, shapes, and colors, started them for a few weeks, and then either lost them, stopped writing in them, or had them borrowed by my youngest daughter, Gracie, who, as a young child, had the annoying habit of taking my notebook, drawing a scribble on every page, and putting it back on the shelf. In my office, notebooks of all sizes, shapes, and colors crowd the shelves. Here is a stack of them.

I have recently begun rereading my failed notebooks, and I have discovered they are not as bad as I had thought they were. There was genuine a sense of play in these pages. Writer Ralph Fletcher says a writer's notebook is similar to the gym where he works out. There are big signs on all the walls, "No Judgment Zone." Perhaps I have been too critical of my notebooks and how I use them.

Here are some of the things I found in my notebooks. You can judge for yourself. On second thought, don't judge, just read.

Sketches of places I've traveled

When I went to a museum in Cairo, I took my sketchbook and did a sketch of Tutankhamen's funeral mask. I usually have a hard time focusing in museums. There is so much to see that it becomes a blur. Bringing my notebook and sketching artifacts forces me to slow down my senses and really experience the art in a direct way that lingers in my memory. Recently, I found this old notebook and was immediately transported to the gleaming gold room at the Egyptian Museum where King Tut's relics lie.

When I left the museum that day, I met a perfume salesman in the street. He kept dabbing drops of jasmine and orange blossom scent on my forearms and telling me each perfume contained 10,000 blossoms worth of scent per ounce. As I am a total sucker for a great bargain and a naive tourist, so I followed him to his perfume store where he sold me far more smelly product than anyone could possibly need. Later that day, when my friend informed me I had purchased cheap chemical perfume thinking it was essence of jasmine flower, I did a sketch of me in the perfume store. As I did my sketch, I recalled a line from our conversation that summed up the whole afternoon.

"I smelled your perfume," I said to the perfume salesman.

"I smelled your money," he replied.

Sketching memories keeps them in our minds forever.

Sketch I made at the Egyptian Museum

Sketch of me in the perfume store

Lists of stories to write about

Notebooks are great places to write down ideas for books and stories that come to you in a flash. You lose them if you don't write them down. You need to catch them like butterflies. Here are some of mine:

- The taxicab driver who gave me a ride home and told me of the suicide in the next apartment
- A story about Casa Dega, Florida, a community of crazy old lady psychics
- A story about my aunt who returned to Poland from Palestine during World War II and into the Holocaust
- Two brothers who find a mysterious photo in a box in the attic

Wisdom lists

What have you learned about the world? Put it into one sentence. Here are three from Dave Barry:

- "The quality of a movie bears a direct relationship to the number of helicopters appearing in the first two minutes."
- "People who are nice to you but not to the waiter are not nice people."
- "Anything a telemarketer says is free—isn't."

Clippings, photos, and other artifacts

Ralph Fletcher has written three great resources on keeping notebooks: *A Writer's Notebook*, *Breathing In, Breathing Out*, and *Lessons for the Writer's Notebook*. He suggests that we strive to be collective and reflective. Gather the stuff that fascinates you, then spend some time looking back at what you have collected, and see if you get the urge to write. Think artifacts, letters, articles, e-mails, tickets, feathers, locks of baby hair—all these things make great "entries" in a writing notebook and can spur some terrific writing. Notebooks can be like scrapbooks of your life with a reflective component that scrapbooks lack. For example, here is a speeding ticket. Why did I put it in my notebook?

Speeding ticket

The Vermont state trooper invited me back with him to his car to keep him company as he wrote my ticket. He said to me, "You know, if you are going to continue to speed like this, you are really going to need a radar detector." He then proceeded to recommend the right brand for me. I wanted to remember this funny moment, so I enshrined it in my notebook. Teacher Gretchen Bernabei often writes down interesting things her students say in her notebook. Then she asks them, "Will you sign this?"

Newspaper clippings about a dead alligator

It seemed ironic to me that a 65-year-old, 14-foot Florida alligator was shot because he looked menacing. It made me think of all the menacing 65-year-old drivers on Florida roads. Irony is my favorite reason for putting a clipping in my notebook. This clip, which was originally reported in the *Alligator Times*, ended up in my book *51 Wacky We-search Reports*. The headline read: "Senior Citizen Slain!"

Unanswerable questions

The most interesting questions in life don't really have answers. But we spend a lot of time wondering about them. Here are some that made it into my notebooks:

- Where do we go when we die?

- Why was I not born someone else?

- Where do ideas begin?

- Is humanity mostly good or bad?

- How can the world come together when so much is pulling us apart?

- What is peace?

- What can one measly person do to change the world?

Beginnings of books you may never write

A notebook is a great place to start a novel you may never finish. Writing a great lead or opening paragraph is something you can easily practice in your notebook. Who knows, some day you might even decide to write it. Here are some of my leads:

- He never could remember the color of her eyes.

- I have never been able to tell a lie, until now.

- You may not know me. I am not the girl of your nightmares, I am not the girl of your dreams.

Okay. They are not great beginnings, but this is my notebook, my chance to play around.

Life gems and quotes

Your notebook is a place to collect quotations about the world we live in. You can write down quotes you stumble across in your reading, or go to Web sites like www.quotationspage.com to find scores of quotations organized thematically. Here are some quotations I have collected.

- Our lives begin to end the day we become silent about things that matter. —Martin Luther King

- Not all are capable of greatness but all are capable of doing small kindnesses with great love. —Mother Teresa

- A joke that works is complete knowledge in a nanosecond. —Steve Martin

- We need fewer mandates and more blind dates. —Barry Lane

Silly what-ifs

What-ifs are when you imagine the world as different than it is. They come to me usually as a silly idea. You can what-if people, places, events, science, math, anything.

Example:

What if instead of seeking power, money, and status, most people sought humility, moderate wealth, and service to others?

(Here's the part where you try to make your "what-if" true.) A third-class ticket on the plane would have you sitting in the big chairs at the front of the plane and a first-class ticket would have you helping the flight attendants serve the coffee.

What-iffing helps your playful imagination spread its wings.

"Ooh!" facts

When reading nonfiction, we often come across extraordinary facts. Some are so extraordinary that they take our breath away. I call these "ooh!" facts and my notebooks abound with them. Here are a few.

- The population of North America was estimated to be 120 million people in 1491, the year before Columbus arrived.
- The largest Roman bath held 33,000 people.
- Dolphins sleep with one eye open.

Spectacular to-do lists

Nothing like finding an old to-do list and realizing you have done it all. One thing I like to do in my notebooks is mix common to-dos with impossible to-dos. Doing so allows me to:

- Do laundry
- Buy milk
- Bring an end to all war

This way, when I look back on my lists, I will always have something left to do. This sounds kind of silly but whenever I add an uncommon to-do to a grocery list, it helps me to step back from everyday life and see the big picture.

Specific lifetime goals

Self-help writer Jack Canfield says that the more specific we get with our lifetime goals, the more chance they have of coming to fruition. I like to add goals I will never reach to my list. I call this a *NOT* goal list. Writing down goals that others might share helps me to think of my own real goals.

Here are some of my lifetime goals:

- Make at least half of my income from my writing
- Spread joy and humor to teachers
- Be a good father
- Go to India

Here is my *not* list:

- Climb Mount Everest
- Win karaoke contest
- Swim English Channel

Ancestor photos

One way to explore your past in a notebook is to find old photographs and make copies or scans to put in your notebook. Write about what these photos mean to you. This is a photograph of my Great Aunt Rifka, who died in the Holocaust. I have never written about her, but I put this photo in my notebook.

My Great Aunt Rifka

Big connections: Wise, rambling rants about reading

Have you ever read a piece in a newspaper, or seen a play or a movie, or read a novel and suddenly you could see the connections between all things? I call this phenomenon "big connections," and it is my attempt to see a thread that runs through everything.

Notice how when you step back, big connections transcend science and politics and history to create a new understanding. This is also called rambling. By the way, you don't have to agree with me, and if you don't, try writing your own view in your notebook.

All You Need Is Love

The Beatles sang it and it sounds hokey and idealistic, but it is really true. Love is an energy like magnetism or the force in *Star Wars*. It cannot be dominated or controlled, only expressed, and spread around. A dictator can control people through fear, but he can never force people to love him. Love has to be earned. This was proven to me when I witnessed the exact moment the Romanian revolution began in 1990. Dictator Nicolae Ceausescu had paid a crowd to stand in the courtyard and cheer for him as he walked out on the balcony. It was a photo opportunity to help quash the student unrest that had been plaguing the country. He walked out on the balcony and started waving to the enthusiastic supporters he had purchased but their jeers were drowned out by the thousands of students who had come to denounce the dictator. Ceausescu backed away into the room and moments later a helicopter landed on the roof to whisk him away. You can make someone hate you, but you can't make them love you. Maybe that's why in Corinthians 13:13 it says, "And now these three remain: faith, hope and love. But the greatest of these is love." Love is like nothing else.

Bad poems

A few years ago, I entered the Julia A. Moore bad poetry contest at the Flint Public Library. Writing bad poetry is a great assignment for a notebook because the very idea implies that nothing you write counts. Here is one of my bad poems. I entered it in the contest, but it didn't win. Not bad enough.

Ode to a Dental Hygienist

As the sixth month check up draws nigh
My heart beats fast
My molars sigh
For she will scrape at my bicuspids
Like a worker chips at autos rusted
Oh how can I express this urgent need
When so profuse these gums do bleed
And I feel so at a loss
If only each night these teeth I'd flossed.
She asks me now if I'm in pain
As blood drips from my chin like rain
Oh fill this heart with Novocaine
Numb these lips or I'll go insane
And tell her what I really think

As she hovers there
Above the sink.
Rinsing teeth of all my plaque
Oh wretched life,
Oh chair
Go back!

The real point here is that a notebook is a place to play. There are no right answers in your notebook. The more you share playful excerpts from your notebooks, the more your students will know this. So let's get started sharing notebooks with your class. But first, write this on the board: *No right answers.*

TRY THIS!

STARTING A WRITER'S NOTEBOOK

Now it's time to make your own notebook with your class. It's best to start with something simple.

Model It

Bring in a notebook you have kept for a month or so. Modeling how to keep a notebook is the best way to get students excited about keeping their own. Talk to your students about the entries in your notebook. What kind of things will they put in? Make sure you have decorated the cover of your notebook. Tell your students that this book is special place to gather ideas, and to play with writing. A notebook is a playground. Make sure your notebook reflects this playful feeling. They will also use their notebooks for mini-lessons done in class or to reflect on reading assignments.

Make a list of things to write about in your notebook. Here are some things I keep in mine:

- sketches
- places to write about
- question lists
- people to write about
- cartoons
- quotes

- what–ifs
- book blurbs

Do It

Pass out notebooks to students in your class. Get the kind of notebooks with blank covers that can be decorated. Ask them to decorate their notebooks any way they want. Ask students to write whatever they want to write in their notebooks. Spend a good deal of time just making your notebook your own.

Debriefing

How do you feel about having a notebook? What kind of things are you going to put in it?

Once you start a notebook, then it's time to experiment with what to put in it. One of my favorite experiments I learned from a writer of books for young adults named Vicki Grove. She calls her notebook a life catcher, and she uses it to collect dialogues, descriptions, and moments from everyday life.

TRY THIS!
TRYING OUT YOUR LIFE CATCHER

Model It

Author Vicki Grove calls journals life catchers. Discuss with your students how their journals can be a place to observe the world around them and collect impressions, details, dialogue, and characters. Take some to time to collect some pieces from your journal and share them with your students.

Do It

Ask your students to take their journal somewhere in the school with a partner for ten minutes and catch some life in their journal. Report back to the classroom to share the life caught.

Debriefing

Was it hard to find life to put into your journal? Which bit of life do you like the best? What is the advantage for a writer to keep a life catcher?

A Visit to Amsterdam

I arrived at 267 Prinsengracht early on a winter morning back in 1978, before it was a big museum with thousands visiting each day. I was a young man of 23. I climbed the steep staircases to the bookcase on hinges, the hidden entrance to the annex. I was the first one that day, and the sunlight shone through the chestnut trees, the same chestnut trees, and the same sunlight, that Anne Frank saw back in the dark days of 1943.

Being there so early in the day gave me a chance to think about the people whose lives were depicted in *The Diary of Anne Frank*. Anne and Margot, Mr. Van Daan and Albert Dussell, the dentist, and of course, Miep, the Dutch woman who sacrificed so much to help them. I felt particularly close to Anne for two reasons: I was raised Jewish and I was the younger sibling in my family. When I first read her diary back in junior high, I remember being struck by how perceptive Anne was about being the youngest in her family and how she used her diary to reflect not just about daily life in the annex but about the larger, darker world outside. Some lines have stuck with me all these years.

- How wonderful it is that nobody need wait a single moment before starting to improve the world.

- Everyone has inside of him a piece of good news. The good news is that you don't know how great you can be! How much you can love! What you can accomplish! And what your potential is!

- Whoever is happy will make others happy too.

- I still believe, in spite of everything, that people are truly good at heart.

Anne was an eternal optimist and beneath all her adolescent struggles is this wise soul putting it all in perspective. I kept a diary for one year when I was Anne's age but when I read it today, it does not inspire anything like Anne's diary. Here is a typical entry:

> John and Rick came over and we played pool. Rick won and then we went out for pizza. We watched *Bonanza*.

There are pages and pages of mundane events recorded in sparse detail, without the least bit of reflection or connection. It is as though I was a soulless phantom sleepwalking through a consumer society.

When I look back on my diary, I see the same kind of robotic writing I see in classrooms where journal writing is mandated. The students are just recording facts without emotion or reflection.

Tuesday, May 22
The day began with more Cheerios from the same box as Monday.

It's not that these students are boring people; rather they don't know the power of writing to make sense of life. They don't know the skill or the value of stepping back and seeing the big-picture truth of your life. Here are some playful lessons for starting this process and playing with it in the notebook. They won't turn your students into writers at the level of Anne Frank, but they will show them some of Anne's techniques as a diarist. A notebook is a place to play, and, as a teacher, you can encourage this by introducing some games.

The Journal Grind

copyright 2008 Discover Writing Press www.discoverwriting.com

TRY THIS!

THE MOUNTAIN AND THE SEA: THE TWO BASIC MOVES OF WRITING

Whenever you write about anything, you have two main choices. You swim in the sea of life, writing with rich physical detail to draw the reader into an experience, or you climb the mountain of abstraction and gaze down at the patterns of the waves, making sense of it all.

Model It

Talk to your students about two basic modes of writing: 1) in one, you write about experience directly; 2) in the other, you stand back from yourself and make sense of it all. For example, I can write "I sit in the dentist's chair looking up at the ceiling at the grotesque pictures of yellow, rotten teeth, and raw, bleeding gums." Or I can step back and write "My dentist has a bizarre way of encouraging his patients to floss their teeth." The first way pulls the reader in with sensory detail; the second steps back and reflects about an event, trying to make sense of it all. Both kinds of writing help the writer to connect with a reader. The first connects with the reader's senses, the second with the reader's reason. Talk to your students about how a journal is a place to experiment with these two moves.

The Mountain of Abstraction and the Sea of Experience

Do It

1. Ask your students to think of a vivid experience, list a few, then pick one. Next ask them to write about that experience for nine minutes in the first person, present tense. Here is an example:

    I sit in the dentist's chair looking up at the ceiling at the posters of rotting gums. I reach for the plastic cup of mouthwash.

2. Ask your students to read over what they have written so far, skip a few lines, and now write about that same event in the past tense. Here is an example:

    I always loved going to the dentist's office as a kid because the dentist and his staff made you feel you were a special person just because you did something as mind-numbing and simple as flossing your teeth.

Debriefing

What is the difference between these two examples? Which move do you personally feel most comfortable with? How can stepping back help improve your writing? How can stepping back weaken a piece of writing?

WRITE ABOUT AN ANCESTOR

The two moves of writing span genre and mode. In many kinds of nonfiction writing, sensory detail is replaced with facts, which support or prove a truth believed by the writer. In third-person fiction, the author moves between the physical circumstances of a character's life and the thoughts of that character.

Model It

1. Ask your students to bring in a photo of a relative. Some students will bring a picture of their mother or father, but a photo of a grandparent works better. Next, ask your students to paste the photo or a copy of it in their notebook. If you don't have a copy machine, students can also draw a little picture of it in their notebooks. Now take a few minutes and simply describe the picture, in the third person. Here's my description of Great Aunt Rifka:

   "The woman stares intently at the camera. She wears a winter coat with a heavy fur collar around her neck. Her eyes have a blank stare as though she is expecting something to happen beyond the simple click of a camera shutter."

My Great Aunt Rifka

2. Ask your students to stop and read over their descriptions. Have them pretend you can climb inside that person's mind, and write a monologue in the first person about what the person is thinking. Great Aunt Rifka might have been thinking something like this:

   "When he is going to take the picture? I can't believe it is taking this long. I don't even want to go to America, so why am I here?"

3. Read over your monologue. Skip a space and try writing in your own voice, as you reflect on that moment. My reflection on Great Aunt Rifka's photo:

   "When I look at the picture of Rifka, my great aunt who died in the Holocaust even though she had been sent steamship tickets three times by my grandmother, I see a face more afraid of change than of death."

Debriefing

What did it feel like to shift your point of view as a writer? From which point of view were you the most comfortable writing? How can what you learned here help you when you are writing a story?

TRY THIS!

PRACTICING MOVES: THE LULLABY WEAVE

One way to play in a notebook is to play with language structure in a narrative. This is a lesson Gretchen Bernabei taught me. It appears in her book *Reviving the Essay: How to Teach Structure Without Formula* and is one of the best ways I know to create excitement for the sound of language.

Model It

Ask your students to think of a time someone in their family sang to them. If they can't think of one, have them think of a time when they were sitting in the car with someone and a certain song was playing on the radio.

Do It

1. Find a blank page in your journal, draw a line down the middle, and then, skipping lines down the left side of page, write the numbers 1, 3, 5, and 7. On the other side, write the numbers 2, 4, 6, and 8.

2. On the left side, write a short description of the person singing to you or of the song on the radio. On the right side, write some words from the song.

3. Now read the lines in number order. This will weave lines from the song into the description of the person or the moment in the car. Here's my example:

I sit in the car beside my father
> **Fairy tales can come true,**
He lights a Havana cigar and I choke on the smoke
> **It can happen to you.**
It's a cold, crisp November day and he turns to me
> **If you're young at heart.**

Me with my father

Debriefing

What did you think of your lullaby weave? How might you use this technique in a story? Were you surprised how the language sounded when you wove one type of writing into another?

What other kinds of weaving could you do as a writer?

GROWING INSIGHT FROM LITERATURE AND LIFE

Another way to use a notebook is as a petri dish for insights into literature and life. One of the hardest things to teach is how to think deeply. That is because students have to gain insights from their own experience of the world, not some prefab idea a well-meaning teacher or a textbook has. I wrote about this lesson in my first book, *Why We Must Run with Scissors: Voice Lessons in Persuasive Writing 3–12*, coauthored with Gretchen Bernabei. It is one of the most powerful ways I know to lead students to deeper understanding.

Model It

Find a picture that speaks to some truth about the world or illuminates an aspect of the literature you are studying. Under the picture, write a truth about the world.

Do It

1. Ask your students to spend seven minutes writing about the photo and the insight. Do they think it's true? Why, or why not? Stop.

2. Have them write for seven minutes about a movie, book, news item, or event that relates to this picture or truth. Encourage them to connect the photo to the movie or book, or to something in the newspaper or a history book.

3. Students read over what they have written and spend the next seven minutes connecting this photo and truth to something in their own lives.

Debriefing

Ask your students, "When you read over your writing, in which of the three segments did you think you connected best to the photo? How does connecting your thoughts to literature and life improve a piece of writing?"

Maureen and April

Gifts from memory

For the second assignment I wrote about the movie *Midnight Cowboy* with Dustin Hoffman and Jon Voight. It premiered when I was 13, but it was rated X, so I could not go to the theater to see it. Luckily, my Dad, who was smitten with the movie, told me the whole story. The main character was Ratso Rizzo, a homeless man sick with tuberculosis. My dad described a key moment in Ratso's character development. It's when he goes to the cemetery to visit his father's grave. He stands there for a moment or two, then he takes a basket of flowers off another grave and puts it on his father's. Everything Ratso got in life he had to take from someone else. I know why my dad loved that movie. It's because he could have been Ratso Rizzo. You see, my Dad grew up fatherless and penniless in the slums of the Lower East Side of Manhattan. More than once, he stole food to eat, and one day he decided, at the tender age of 9, to spend his day hanging out on the streets instead of going to school. If not for a certain truant officer, my father is convinced he would have turned to crime instead of aspiring to the middle-class life.

The last part of the exercise made me remember my trip to South Africa. We were in the van, on the way back to the Holiday Inn Green Park in Cape Town. I was with eight teachers from St. Louis and we had just said goodbye to the most amazing South African teachers, with whom we had worked for a week in a retreat. We were filled with that kind of sweet sadness you only get when you say goodbye to people you have just met but feel like you have known a lifetime. It had been a very special week for all of us. We had planned to do some shopping for souvenirs at the Green Park market and pack for the flight in the morning.

But when the van dropped us off in front of the Holiday Inn, there was a young woman with a baby. She was holding a Styrofoam coffee cup and begging for money. Beside her was a little girl of 8. My friends all got off the bus and headed in different directions, but I had an experience I had not had before and have not had since—I could not move past the woman holding the baby and the little girl. I reached for my wallet and realized I had little cash to give them, so I did the first thing that came to mind. I asked them to join me at the Holiday Inn restaurant for lunch. They gave me a sort of bewildered look when I told them to wait there.

A moment later I had secured a table at the fancy restaurant and waved them in through the exit door. I found out the woman's name was Maureen and her baby's name was Monica. The little girl was April, and she was her next-door neighbor's child. Maureen, who was probably no more than 30 but looked 50, told me that her husband had died in a train accident. A commuter train had hit him. This was a big problem in the Cape flats since all the work was in the city and all the people lived in squatters' shacks miles away. Trains and VW bus taxis carry far too many people and accidents are many. She told me that begging was the only way she could feed her baby.

As Maureen spoke, Monica (who was 2 years old) squirted guava juice at me through a straw. The waiter, a young white male South African named Jonathan, seemed curious and a bit suspicious about my new friends as I introduced Maureen, Monica, and April to him. We spent two hours eating fish and chips and salad. We ordered more food than they could eat, so we packed it all up in to-go boxes for the road. I thanked them for having lunch with me and gave them some cash so they could take the train home. Before we left, Maureen smiled at me. Though she only seemed to have three teeth, it was the most radiant smile I had ever seen.

As I watched them walk away into the marketplace, I realized it wasn't really the food or the money that made Maureen so happy—it was the recognition I gave her as a human being. I also realized the market had closed and I could not do the gift shopping I wanted to. But it didn't matter, because Maureen had given me the greatest gift of all, the knowledge of why we are here. Sharing even a piece of that with my friends back home would be much better than a wood carving or tablecloth.

I am sharing Maureen's gift right now with you. I hadn't planned to, but her memory sprang like a miracle into my notebook. Creating opportunities for these types of miracles is what writing teachers do in all subjects and grade levels.

"YEAH, BUT . . ."
Readers' Questions Answered

How can I teach notebooks when we don't have enough time to do daily writing?

If we accept that writing is thinking and notebooks are a great place to think, your question comes down to, "We don't have enough time to think today in school?" and you are probably right. My response is that we need to add by subtracting. Look at your schedule and see if you can find places to integrate notebook writing into science, math, social studies. Notebooks can be a place to gather thoughts, explore reading assignments, gather ideas for writing assignments, and do mini-lessons and draft essays and stories. A notebook is also a place just to play and explore. See notebooks as much more than an assignment. They are a way of life. For a detailed look at using notebooks in all subjects, I recommend the book *Notebook Know-How* by Aimee Buckner.

How do I grade writing notebooks? How do you grade a student's thoughts?

I don't recommend giving students' notebooks a letter grade. You are simply looking for signs of life. A stronger notebook will have more writing in it and show evidence of daily writing. A weaker notebook might be a bit thinner and only include assignments done in class. Your goal is to encourage students to use their notebooks more, not to rank how they use them. A notebook is a thinking tool, and you want to avoid seeing it as a product. I suggest using checkmarks instead of grades, if you want to do some assessment of your students' notebooks.

I teach history and science. How can I use writers' notebooks as a part of these classes?

No matter what subject you teach, a writer's notebook can be a marvelous unpaid teacher's aide in your class. In history class, you might have your students record their own thoughts about history in their journals. Before giving a reading assignment, ask students to reflect on a question in their journal that prepares them to better understand the reading. This type of educational foreshadowing is sometimes called an anticipation guide because it helps the writer to anticipate what he or she is about to learn. On the funnier side you can do assignments where your student assumes the personality of a character from history or science. Here is an excerpt from the journal of a cheetah, from my book *51 Wacky We-search Reports*. "The lions are here again. Why can't we all be just friends and share the kill? I propose my idea to the head lion. He thinks about it for three seconds then tries to play tetherball with my head. Lions are mean but cheetahs are fast. See ya later, shaggy head!"

CHAPTER 5

ONE WRITER'S WORKSHOP TO GO, TOMORROW

A teacher at one of my workshops once informed me that she didn't write with her students because she was insecure about her own writing. I remember telling her that her insecurity about writing was probably the best thing she could share with her students because it gave them permission to be insecure, too. Imagine, if you will, a pottery class. The students are all at wheels with muddy lumps of clay and the teacher struts around proudly holding a perfect vase, pointing to the students' efforts, and delivering comments like "close." When the students ask her if she has ever made a pot, she replies, "I tried it once. It was a little messy." This teacher would not have much authority as a teacher of pottery.

> A writer is working when he's staring out of the window.
>
> —*Burton Rascoe*

CLOSE.

The Questionable Pottery Teacher

The same holds true for what's known as writer's workshop. A teacher won't be an effective leader of writer's workshop unless he or she is willing to get messy, and be open about his or her own writing struggles with the students. But in recent years, there has been some confusion about what a writer's workshop is and what it can be.

What Is a Writer's Workshop?

Here is my definition of writer's workshop:

> A writer's workshop is a block of time during class designed so that students create and give themselves writing assignments, working hard to improve their writing in cooperation with their peers and their teacher.

This definition does not mean that teachers are not allowed to assign writing subjects or give ideas on how to write. It only means that it's not a writer's workshop if teachers are the only people choosing all the assignments.

Why Do Teachers Resist Giving Their Students Choice?

It has always puzzled me why some teachers have such a hard time giving writing choice to students. In all my years in public school, I never really had a teacher who just allowed us to write regularly on topics of choice. It seemed as if we were always being asked to write according to certain rules or told what our story topics should be. It was as if writing was too important a thing to be left to the imagination of a mere student, and the problem continues to this day; my daughters have had similar experiences. Business guru Tom Peters says, "Our school system is a thinly disguised conspiracy to quash creativity."

I think Peters is onto something, but there are also good, legitimate reasons why teachers fear and avoid student choice. Here are a few of the top ones.

Students might write about inappropriate topics.

Remember my seventh-grade teacher, Mrs. Kent, who, after reading my parody of the assistant principal's latest speech, said to me, "He might get the wrong idea about the kinds of assignments I'm giving"? If you feel personally responsible for every word your students write, you are going to have trouble with choice. The best writing often is a little edgy. It can straddle the border of "appropriate." I can remember many times when a student handed me an assignment prefaced with the words, "I probably shouldn't hand this to an

English teacher," and it was the student's best work. When students have choice, they take risks, and we can reward them or gently caution them if they go too far. But if we don't give them a chance to experiment, they will keep their true selves out of their writing.

Students might write about video games or TV or other popular schlock culture.

This is one I hear often. Students' minds are teeming with popular culture, and when they write they can often describe what they see on TV or in video games. The answer here is simple: They are writing about the world they know, and they may need to start there. A video game is a story, with characters and obstacles that get in the way of their dreams. An assignment might be to take a novel you are reading in class and turn it into a video game. I guarantee some of your less motivated students will excel at this assignment and will enjoy the chance to strut their Nintendo stuff. It's also worth studying the complexity of video games so that we understand the positive side to them. Ask your students what a novel like *Charlotte's Web* might look like as a video game.

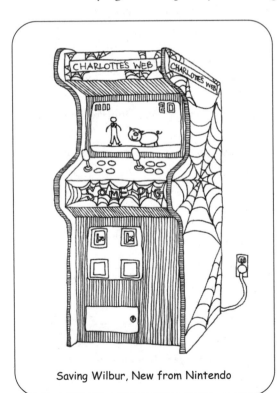

Saving Wilbur, New from Nintendo

Students might write about personal or family trauma.

It is inevitable that students will talk about painful things in their writing, and sometimes this may even compel you by law to speak with a counselor at your school. A high school journal from English class is often the bridge between a troubled soul and the school system and society. Some teachers ask students to fold over a page in their journal that they don't want the teacher to read. This simple method can protect a student's privacy and give them a choice to share or not. My experience has been that students in pain want and need to share it with someone. Keeping choice out of your classroom may protect you from having to wear a counselor hat once in a while, but it also might reinforce the idea that there is no one in the larger society interested in your students' emotional reality. Being in school is sometimes like being invisible. A troubled student may feel unseen and unknown.

They will write about violence.

Since the Columbine and Virginia Tech shootings, the role of violence in teens' writing, particularly boys', has become a national issue. I believe a teacher has the absolute right to ask her students not to write about violence in a graphic manner, but be careful about making any general class rules that stop a student from writing, period. Ask yourself if your fear of students' writing about violent subjects is what is stopping you from allowing choice in your classroom. If it is, ask yourself what you are afraid of. You might find the answer is not the violence in your students' writing, but the violence in the world at large. Allowing choice writing enables students to face these issues head on and become more conscious of these negative influences in their lives. Choice writing opens a dialogue, and dialogue offers the possibility of change.

MY LIFE CHANGED THE DAY I GOT MY GLUE GUN

I hope I have convinced you to start some form of writer's workshop. You have time and space and you are ready for some choice. Where do you begin? How do you keep it going? And what do you need to keep your job, in case your administrator does not understand why you are sitting and writing with your students when you should be teaching?

Let's begin by saying there is no one way to begin a writer's workshop and no one way to structure it, but there are some general guidelines and forms to help you create your own structure. Teachers moving from a traditional model of being a sage on the stage to a more modern design of being a guide on the side need a different type of organizational structure that is more imbedded in the class. We will need some forms to help us keep track of it all, and I provide examples in this chapter. My favorite quote by a teacher was told to me by my friend Jim Defillippi. He had overheard a woman say this and he knew she must be a teacher: "My life changed the day I got my glue gun."

This chapter is your glue gun. I hope I can give you enough glue to hold your writing workshop together until it takes on a life of its own.

Dividing Your Time

A writer's workshop might be divided into three slices of varying sizes:

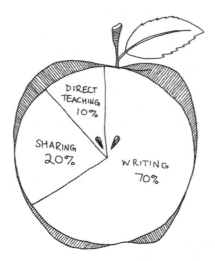

You can mess with the proportions, but the main point is that writing is first, sharing is second, and teaching has the least time allotted. The idea here is that we learn to write by writing and that teaching and sharing serve writing.

So let's take a minute and define the components of a writer's workshop.

The mini-lesson

A mini-lesson can come at the beginning of a writing block or at the end of a writing block. The goals of a mini-lesson can be different but the format is a 15-minute taste of teaching that helps students move forward in their writing and thinking. For example, a mini-lesson can be as simple as reading a poem to your students, and then asking them to think about the poem and how it inspires them to write a similar poem. Another mini-lesson might be to take an aspect of the craft from literature and have students try to imitate that craft idea in their notebooks. Another idea might be to learn about a point of grammar and experiment with it in a few sentences in the notebook. Effective teachers take cues from their students on the content of a mini-lesson. For example, when you see that a few students are having trouble finding a meaningful topic, create a lesson to address the problem.

A regular writing time

This is the time when the students write, and it is your job to get out of the way. One of the best ways to do this is to write yourself, with your students, but that might not always be possible in a class where some students need your assistance and quiet motivation. Here are some suggestions for low-key teacher activities during the writing portion of writer's workshop.

- Use the first five minutes of a writing block to check in and connect with each student. Ask *How are you? Where are you in your writing?* A student may need to tell you what happened on the bus that day.

- Confer with an individual or with a small group.

- Write an inspiring quote on the board that might help a student who is stuck.

- Remember: No matter how long or how short your writing time is, make sure it's at a regularly scheduled time so that students can expect it and plan for it.

Sharing time

When I first started working with adults, I once started a writing workshop by asking the participants to write down a secret they had never told anyone. Five people immediately headed for the door. One hand shot up.

"Do I have to share with anybody?" I thought for a moment and said, "No, only one person, yourself."

Sharing is an important part of a writer's workshop but should not be mandatory. Knowing you don't have to share frees you to write, and, oddly enough, more students end up wanting to share. There are many ways to set up sharing. Here are a few of my favorites:

- Have students come to the front of the room five at a time. Each reads his or her piece and stays there until all five have read. This is good public speaking practice, and it's less intimidating to stand with others.

- Get a small PA and a wireless microphone. Then go around the room Oprah-style and have students read their piece into the microphone. This is a great way to do a quick share, and I haven't met a student yet who didn't love talking into a microphone. In fact, if you can't afford a mic, just get the inside of a roll of toilet paper and pretend to use it as a mic. Students will talk even louder to simulate the mic effect.

- Use an author's "share chair." Each writing block, a student sits in it, and shares his or her piece. This is not a writing conference because no critical comments are made. This is simply a time to listen and acknowledge.

Celebrating time

Unlike sharing time, which might occur every day, celebrating time happens on days when something special happens, such as when a student achieves a longed-for goal and when time permits.

Writing conferences

A writing conference is a chance for the teacher and students to read beyond the text and see what lies beneath. In a traditional writing class, teachers commented directly on students' papers and assumed they knew the intent of the writer. In conferences writers have a chance to reveal what they were shooting for. Teachers can guide writing conferences with full-group instruction and focus writing conferences on particular aspects of the craft—or even grammar. See more detailed information on writing conferences later in this chapter.

Writing folders and writing portfolios

- A writing folder is a place where students gather all their work.

- A writing portfolio is a folder that contains what students have selected as their best work. Along with their work, which is often self-evaluated, students write an explanation of why they chose each piece.

Keeping track of it all: Imbedding structure

A teacher moving from a more traditional teaching structure to a writer's workshop might be intimidated by the lack of structure in a writing workshop.

For example, if the teacher doesn't "collect and correct," how does she know students are working?

A traditional writing class is like a Roman battleship from the movie *Ben Hur*, where the student crew is chained to the oars as the teacher coxswain calls out the assignments. A writer's workshop is more like a sailing crew. Here a captain calls out the orders and each crew has a job to execute to keep the vessel moving. After a while the crew knows the jobs and can operate the ship without the captain on deck. The crew takes on a life of its own. Students know what they need to do and time becomes a commodity. Setting up a class that runs on its own requires work and time.

The assignment-giving classroom

The Many Faces of Writer's Workshop

Maybe you are not ready to jump into a full-blown writer's workshop. Maybe you don't have the time. You teach history, science, math. You have stuff to teach, content to test. Your curriculum tells you you have to use a certain program, yadda, yadda, yadda. Let me show you some simple ways to build choice writing into your crowded teaching life.

The seven-minute writing workshop

The writing classroom

copyright 2008 Discover Writing Press www.discoverwriting.com

Take the first seven minutes of each and every class and have the students write. Direct their writing with a quote on the board, but give them the freedom to stray off the topic or continue writing in their notebooks about last week's quote. Eventually, after several weeks, ask them to develop one piece from their notebooks into a finished essay or story.

Writing Mondays

I learned this from my friend Deborah Craig, a fourth-grade teacher in a school that used to do a full-blown writer's workshop. With so many assessments and specials, it was too hard to find time for choice writing. So rather than give it up entirely, Monday is now choice writing day. Students write letters to Deborah and she responds. They call it Writing Mondays, and all the kids look forward to it.

The one-day-a-week writer's workshop

Here, a teacher takes one entire period or, in elementary school, an entire day and just invites the students to write. This is Writing Day, and if you can find a way to pull this off, I believe you will have a much better chance of creating a writing classroom, even in a school environment that seems to discourage writing and thinking. To make this successful, find ways to create a sense of anticipation for Writing Day. Have your students take a few minutes during the week to write in their notebooks and make sure they come to Writing Day with something to write about.

FROM RED INK TO REAL TALK: LEARNING THE ART OF CONFERRING

Reese Haller

Reese Haller is a fifth grader from Michigan who has written several books about Fred the Mouse. His publisher calls him the world's youngest author. I met him in the hall at the Michigan Reading Association. He was speaking that afternoon on the eight secrets of good writing. I introduced myself and told him I could not attend his talk, but I asked him if he could just tell me the first secret. He paused for a moment and then his eyes widened and a big smile spread across his face. "That's easy," he said. "Believe."

Reese described what I think is the most important thing about writing conferences, for they provide a chance for a writer to believe he has something to say and a chance for the teacher or a peer to promote that belief. Everything else that occurs is just gravy. I learned this first from Donald Murray when I taught at the University of New Hampshire. Murray was famous for saying very little during a writing conference. Instead, he let the writer talk about the work. He would sometimes ask questions or offer a suggestion based on his own experience as a writer, but more often than not he just sat back and listened. But it was not passive listening. Anyone who met with Murray knew this. Murray's listening helped you to find your own way. Murray was the perfect audience.

Writer Brenda Ueland once described the importance of listening in an essay. "Who are the people you go to for advice? Not to the hard, practical ones who can tell you exactly what to do, but to the listeners; that is, the kindest, least censorious, least bossy people that you know. It is because by pouring out your problem to them, you then know what to do about it yourself."

Donald Murray listening

TRY THIS!
WHAT IS A HELPFUL CRITIC?

Let's get this straight from the start: Being a helpful critic is not just a writing skill, it is a life skill. If you can offer a friend honest insight in a gentle way that does not impose burden or a sense of failure, you possess a very important social skill. This lesson starts a process I never learned when I was in school: how to be a helpful critic.

Model It

Ask your students, "What is a helpful critic? Talk to your students about what makes a helpful critic. Ask them, "Do you have a helpful critic in your life? What kind of things do helpful critics do?"

Do It

1. Make a list of some of these qualities. Helpful critics:

    *   Listen

    *   Start with something positive

    *   Ask curious questions

    *   Are honest but kind

    *   Offer one suggestion

    *   Make you want to write more

2. Post your list in the classroom.

Debriefing

What is the most important quality on the list? How can this list help with other things besides writing? What makes a writing conference work for you? Can you add any more qualities of helpful critics to the list?

A NEW PATTERN OF COMMUNICATION BETWEEN TEACHER AND STUDENT

Comedian Jerry Seinfeld has a bit that touches on the problem with the traditional way writing teachers and students communicated. He says,

> "I always did well on essay tests, just put everything you know in there and maybe you'll hit it. Then you get the paper back from the teacher. One word scrawled across the entire page: VAGUE. I thought that was a vague thing to say. I crossed it out and wrote UNCLEAR and sent it back. She sent it back to me, HAZY. I sent it back to her, MUDDY. We are still corresponding to this day. CLOUDY . . . AMBIGUOUS."
>
> —*SeinLanguage*

A real writing conference is a chance to escape this holding pattern of miscommunication. Here are my best tips for improving your conferences with students. For more, read Carl Anderson's book *How's It Going?: A Practical Guide to Conferring With Student Writers.*

Barry's Top Ten Tips for Teacher-Student Conferences

10. Make sure the student speaks first about his or her writing. It's like tennis. The serve controls the game. Carl Anderson's book *How's It Going?* gives you your cue right in the title.

9. Practice active, curious listening. Withhold comments and snap judgments.

8. When you get bogged down, turn the paper over and talk about the subject off the page: "Tell me more about your aunt who died."

7. Ask clarifying questions rather than offer prescriptions. Instead of "Do this," try "What would happen if you did this?"

6. Encourage genre-hopping: "What would happen if you turned this into a poem?"

5. Praise specifically. Instead of "I liked it," say "I love the part where you are trying to decide what to do and you start listing ideas in your mind."

4. Separate grammar conferences from content conferences, and focus grammatical conferences on key problem areas.

3. When possible, share your own experiences as a writer if you think it will help students improve their writing. "I wrote a story like that once . . ." .

2. When possible, direct students to literature that models and teaches. Dav Pilkey's books might give you an idea of what you are shooting for.

1. Offer one suggestion but always give students a chance to define their own direction first. "So where are you going with this?"

TRY THIS!

START A WRITING WORKSHOP TOMORROW

After skimming this chapter, you should have the tools to start your own writer's workshop, no matter what grade or subject you teach. Here's a way to get started.

Model It

Start by getting out a calendar and lesson plan book and blocking writing times for your students. Decide how you are going to work the writer's workshop time into each week along with the other requirements of your curriculum. Use some of the tools provided in this chapter to help you and your students organize the writing time.

Debriefing

Was it hard to find writing time? Do you feel as if you are giving up more important instructional time? How can you add choice writing to content-driven assignments?

"YEAH, BUT . . ."

Readers' Questions Answered

How can I teach using a writing workshop approach when I have so much content to cover in my biology class? This is really just for language arts teachers, right?

Wrong. A writer's workshop can be as big or as small as you want it to be. For example, I met a physics teacher in college who had his students scribble a five-minute note at the end of each lecture about what they had learned. He used these comments to gauge his teaching. If the students had kept these notes, it would be the beginning of a writer's workshop. The next step might be to have his physics students keep a physics journal where they write comments at the beginning of each class about what they will be learning. Perhaps the teacher might have a question or quote on the board about the lesson of the day or the reading. Eventually, one of these brief, in-class journal entries could turn into a paper. Design your writing workshop to meet your needs.

I want to develop a writing workshop but everybody in my school is following a scripted writing program. How can I do the program and keep my job?

This is where I become your mother. If everyone in your school jumped off a cliff, would you jump, too? Scripted writing programs always have names with the word *power* in the title and promise to empower students as writers and create powerful writers. Most of these programs take ideas from 1950s textbooks and simply recycle them for the 21st century. They focus mostly on the structure of writing and produce writers who all create the same paragraphs. These programs often come heavily touted, with expensive double-blind research studies that show how the program has raised test scores in low-performing schools. What they don't tell you is that student's attitudes toward writing take a nosedive in these same schools, and unless the test is particularly weighted toward organization, writing scores rarely top the mediocre level. Writing is thinking, so when you create robot writers, you create robot thinkers. Surely your administrator does not want that. If possible, explain this to him or her. Chances are he will agree as long as you keep it quiet. A real educational leader understands the true value of a creative teacher, and will probably allow some experimentation with different approaches to reach the same goal. But maybe your principal is not a real educational leader. The second approach is to close your door and teach writing in your own way, using the textbook when you see fit. Fly under the radar.

When I tried to start a writing workshop, my students resisted. They are used to being told what to write about. How do I get them to embrace the idea of choice writing?

This is common in schools where students have not been given choice. Students want to be told what to write about. It is important to wait them out. Spend a week or two just gathering ideas to write about. Make lists with them. Tell them stories. Pass around the story stick. Remember that talking is the first language, drawing the second, and writing the third. Start with the first language and move to the second. One idea: Write about a shared experience such as the first day of school. Talk about your feelings that day. Draw a picture. Write about it. The talking and the drawing often bring the writing into focus. Chances are, if your students have stalled, they have not yet given themselves permission to write. Remember this and find your own ways to accomplish your goal.

There is a line at my desk all the time. Students all want to confer with me. What do I do?

This is a common problem in a class where the teacher is still the big cheese. Here are a few favorite approaches: Show them the do-it-yourself teacher conference and have them write the dialogue of a conversation between you and them. Require that they meet with others before they come to see you. Meet with all students at once. Eventually, as your students become better readers of one another's work, you will become less important.

We have a tight schedule of standards that must be assessed once per quarter. Each quarter, students must write to a prompt. How do you incorporate writing to a prompt into writer's workshop?

One dinky writing prompt per quarter is not a reason to short-circuit real choice writing. I assume that this dreaded writing prompt might address a different writing standard or genre like, for example, persuasive writing. You might want to include a mini-lesson or two on this genre to spice up your writing workshop that month. One of my favorite persuasive writing lessons is from my book *Why We Must Run With Scissors*. The lesson is called "Dressing as the Enemy" and it teaches students to argue their point by taking the side of their opponent. Example, "School uniforms are great. Some of the most important and glorious societies in history have valued the uniform. Take Nazi Germany for example . . . ."

What do you do with kids who are always thinking and never writing?

This can be a tough one. I like to encourage "free staring" as part of the writing process, but you can't have kids staring into space for weeks on end. At some point they have to write something. Kids who stare too much are most likely afraid of writing. I suggest breaking the cycle by doing pencils-up quick-writes with your class on a regular basis. I learned this from author Geof Hewitt in his book *Hewitt's Guide to Slam Poetry and Poetry Slam*. Hewitt sets a timer, holds his pencil high in the air with the rest of the class, and shouts, "Go!" A prize goes to whoever writes the most words in seven minutes. This type of activity will give that starer some fluency.

What do you do with the kids who always say, "I don't know what to write about"?

This is actually a good sign. Tell them that you love it that they are not just going to write any old thing to please you or to get a good grade. You are proud of them for taking writing seriously. Ask them to share ideas from their notebook with a partner. What are they thinking of writing about? Refer back to mini-lessons you have taught or books they have read. Share with them your own struggles to find ideas to write about and maybe pair them with another student who is also having trouble finding topics. Ideas come as students feel free to explore them. I have found that most students who don't know what to write about really do; they just lack the confidence to set words to paper.

How do you help administrators get it?

The answer to this question has changed in the last few years since the federal government got into the business of managing school curricula. Up to that point, teaching was an art; now it has been declared a science. The same kinds of double-blind studies used by pharmaceutical companies to confirm the efficacy of drugs are used to prove the validity of reading and writing programs. Administrators have been told to pay more attention to this data generated in prefab data factories miles away from real classrooms than to the teacher and students in their own building. Only real educational leaders have had the courage to say—like Jimmy Stewart did in the classic Capra film *It's a Wonderful Life* when he is being bought out by the evil, greedy banker—"Now wait just a minute, Mr. Potter."

Most principals, even those who are misinformed and seduced by programs that promise the world, want students to succeed. Your best way to help them understand this is by explaining to them what you are doing and asking for their courageous support. If they want research on the methods presented in this book, direct them to the study posted in the Teacher Center at my Web site, www.discover-writing.com/teachercenter.html. May the force be with you, Luke!

PART II

REASONS TO WRITE

If we had to say what writing is, we would define it essentially as an act of courage.

—*Cynthia Ozick*

CHAPTER 6

STORY MATTERS

Using Narrative Structure to Teach All Writing and Succeed in Life

Mary was a student in my freshman English class, and she had written an essay about a lost friendship in seventh grade. The girl's name was Laura, and Mary had befriended her and invited her into her clique of girlfriends. When Mary returned from a vacation with her family, Laura had taken over the group. All the girls in the group were wearing a new style of shoe and none of them would even speak to Mary. Mary was angry and humiliated and spent the rest of the year an outcast. Then the story jumps ahead a few years. Laura had moved away and Mary was a senior and once again a popular girl. One day, a new student appeared in class. It was Laura. She had moved back from Ohio and now was a new kid with no friends. At the end of the five-page essay, she makes an overture to Mary after math class in the hall, but Mary just sneers at her and walks away.

When I met with Mary in a writing conference I tried to see if she felt even a speck of remorse for her behavior toward Laura, but in her mind, Laura had it coming to her and Mary had waited five years to give it back. It was clear this was not going to be an inspiring essay about forgiveness because Mary had not matured to the point where she could forgive Laura for what she had done back in junior high. The moral to the story would be the all-too-familiar adage: "What goes around comes around."

If this were a fictional story, I don't think Mary would have been a very interesting character because she is the same at the beginning of the story as she

> Story is to human beings what the pearl is to the oyster.
>
> —*Joseph Gold*

is at the end. Neither she, nor Laura, comes to any mature understanding of herself or the world.

Interesting characters change over time. They surprise us, delight us, and scare us, and they go after dreams; they take chances; they seek something and often come away with new self-knowledge.

LANE'S FIRST RULE OF STORIES

An interesting story without an interesting character is not an interesting story.

You can take away the setting and the plot, and you still might have a story, but take away the character and you have nothing of interest. One mistake made by young writers and experienced movie makers (who should know better) alike is to put their faith in stories, settings, and special effects instead of characters to provide the main interest of the story. In this chapter we are going to learn how to grow stories from characters, and how great stories and narrative technique are not just the domain of fiction writing.

The best way to understand stories is to tell stories in class. One problem with school is that we often use the wrong language. A teacher once asked me, "How do you get kids to write personal narratives?"

Step one: Don't call it a personal narrative.

copyright 2008 Discover Writing Press www.discoverwriting.com

Here is the best way I know to learn about nonfiction stories.

THE STORY CIRCLE

A story circle is a very natural way of generating stories with your class. If you have ever asked your students to write about their lives and been told that their lives are boring, this is a great lesson to try with them.

Model It

Gather your desks, or students, in one large circle or many small circles. Either can work, depending on who you are or who your students are. Tell your students that stories are everywhere, but that the way to find stories is to tell stories.

You might introduce the story circle this way: If someone asks me to tell a story, I go blank, but if you tell a story, I think of a story. Today we are going to tell and find them.

In life we do a ritual called conversation. That's when you tell a story and I interrupt you, or I tell a story and you interrupt me. Today we are going to try a new ritual. It comes from Native American culture and it's called the talking stick. I am going to tell a story and you are going to listen. The only person who gets to talk is the person holding the talking stick. We are going to pass the stick around the room and tell stories. I am going to start with a story from my life. (Tell a story and pass the stick.)

Debriefing

Was it hard to think of a story to tell? Did other people's stories make you think of more stories? What makes a story interesting? What makes a story boring? How does what we learned about our own stories apply to stories in books?

THE LIFE CLASS

It is the middle of winter and I am flat broke. I notice an ad in the newspaper for a life model. It pays $10 an hour, which is a lot of money to me. All you have to do is stand naked in front of a class of artists while they sketch you for a few hours. Piece of cake, I think, and apply for the job. I get it and am asked to return in a week.

A week goes by and suddenly I start to really think about what it will be like to stand naked, in the middle of January, in front of a group of students as they draw me. I wake up in the middle of the night in a cold sweat. Will they laugh at me? Will I be able to stand there without cracking up myself? Will I turn red in embarrassment?

The day arrives and I get an idea. My idea is this. I will not be naked. I will be nude, like the Greek sculptures I have seen in art history classes, and in Kenneth Clark's film *Civilization*. By striking a pose like the dying Gaul, I will stave off any attempt to see myself as a broke, sad, naked man.

I get to the class, and it's all young women with gigantic pads of paper. There is a partition behind which I am supposed to take off my clothes. I find it odd that even though I am about to stand naked before these women, I still need privacy to take off my clothes. In my mind, I decide this partition is like Superman's phone booth. I will emerge transformed into Super-Nude Model, an ancient Greek sculpture that lives and breathes today.

I begin my first pose, the javelin thrower; then I hurl the discus. To my amazement, there is no tittering, no guffawing, not even a conspiratorial whisper. Only the sound of charcoal scraping paper and the occasional neutral comments of the teacher. "Try showing that negative space." "Notice the line of the figure's jaw." I am the figure and they are art students. What was I so worried about?

A month later, after the job has ended, I stand in the bank, about to withdraw the last of the money from my savings account. I am embarrassed about this because as a young boy a teller once scolded me for taking money out of my savings account. When I reach the teller, she smiles at me when I hand her my passbook. But it's not just a friendly smile, it's a sort of all-knowing, Mona Lisa smile. "I know you," she says. In that one terrible moment, as I stand there in winter coat and scarf, long underwear and flannel shirt, I am totally naked.

"The life class," she says, still smiling, as she hands me the cancelled passbook.

THE GARBAGE MAN IN THE THRONE ROOM

I have told that story to audiences but had never written it down until now. I like that I start off so sure of myself then lose confidence just before the life class, then gain confidence again, then lose confidence again finally in the bank. This shift in attitude is what makes the story funny, but it also illustrates a fundamental premise for creating interesting characters: they have to be capable of changing. They have to surprise us.

One way characters surprise us is by wanting more than they were born with. I learned this years ago in a clown workshop run by the famous comedian known professionally as Avner the Eccentric. Avner, who had just finished his one-man mime show on Broadway, taught us the fundamental premise of all comedic characters.

He began the workshop by asking us to walk around the room shaking hands with one another. Then he talked about how the natural distance people keep between each other is an arm's length. He then said there were two basic types of characters—high-status folks, who hold their heads up and keep their distance, and low-status folks, whose shoulders slump forward and are always in your face. To use psychologist jargon, high-status folks have boundaries, low-status folks do not. What makes a low-status character like Charlie Chaplin's tramp interesting is that he does not see himself as low status. He has dreams. Avner used the classic story of the garbageman in the throne room.

A garbageman comes to the royal palace to collect money for his work. He is told to wait in the throne room for his money. There he is, totally alone in the throne room, staring at the throne and the king's crown, which sits on it. Before long his imagination gets the best of him. What would it feel like to be king? He inches his way to the throne, picks up the crown, and is just about to place it on his head when, suddenly, the door opens.

Avner described this as the rise and the fall. That moment when the door opens is the biggest laugh. He talked about how all the humor on the *I Love Lucy* show rested in that one moment when Lucy's character was found out and fell from the status she had usurped through her trickery. Much of the humor in *I Love Lucy* stemmed from a society that gave no status to women. Lucy dressed as a man and used other tricks to steal some status, but in the end she is always found out and that's where the biggest laughs lie. We laugh at her ingenuity, and even though she is foiled in the end, we don't despair because we look forward to her next predicament.

Garbage man in the throne room

Here is my favorite lesson for teaching this rule of character to students.

TRY THIS!

GROWING A STORY FROM A CHARACTER

Interesting stories have interesting characters, but student's characters are often controlled by the plot. How do we grow a story from a character?

Model It

1. Ask your students what makes an interesting character in a story. Talk about the main character in the story you are reading or simply take a character out of a fairy tale, cartoon, or other story.

    Interesting characters all share one thing: trouble. They have a problem, something they must confront and deal with. But they also share something else. Call it dreams, call it goals. They have to want something, or else the story is dead.

    If Jack decides he is afraid of heights and won't climb the beanstalk, is that an interesting story? Maybe Bugs Bunny decides not to trick Elmer Fudd but just runs from him. Is he an interesting character now? And Hamlet? He decides to ignore his father's ghost, and just live the normal life of a Danish prince, son of his uncle and mother. Would anyone want to read about the well-adjusted Hamlet?

    Great characters don't know their place. They want more. They dream.

    Character = Trouble + Dreams

2. Ask students to work with a partner to create a character who has some kind of trouble that a student in your school might have.

    Do this as a web diagram or a list of qualities. Develop the character with a partner by asking questions about the character. Some questions might be "How old is he?" or "Does he have brothers and sisters?" Others might be more personal, like "What is his trouble?"

Sometimes I model a character for the students. I start with the trouble and ask them to ask me questions.

Examples:

"My name is Tony and I am always in the principal's office."

"My name is Sarah and I'm flunking science."

As the students ask me questions, I point out to them that I don't know the answers to the questions until I hear them. We are creating this character together.

3. After students have created their characters, I introduce them by the name of their characters, and they answer the class's questions for a few minutes. They begin by introducing themselves and briefly describing their problem. The questions posed by the class help to develop each character. Example of a student intro:

"My name is Ashley and I'm popular but no one likes me."

The class asks Seth questions and I write all of them down. After the press conference, I hand them to Seth. Sometimes, by doing this, we see beneath a character to the real problem.

Example:

Class: Why is that?

Student: I have no close friends, even though everyone thinks I do. Maybe I need to be nicer.

Note: It's easier to find the trouble of a character than it is to find the dream. I tell students to start with the trouble and let the dream emerge as they continue thinking and writing about their character.

Debriefing

Was it easy to create a character? Did your character get more interesting the more we asked questions? Did your character get silly and far-fetched, or were you able to keep his problems real? Do you want to write about your character? Is your character high status or low?

WHAT-IFFING THE TROUBLE AND THE DREAM AND CREATING THE OBSTACLE

One advantage to fiction writing is that you get to question everything. What-iffing is a great habit of thinking to model with your class. Here is how to do it.

Model It

Talk to your students about how fiction writers work to create better characters. Ask them if they think their characters are interesting enough. Open the discussion with this question: What makes a character interesting?

Answer: Trouble and dreams. But what if the trouble is not that compelling? Let's say my character's trouble is that his pen leaked in his pants. Is that enough trouble for a story? Probably not, unless these are the only pants he owns and he is a new kid, going to a school for the first time, and the pants are white so everyone can see the big blue stain, but who wears white pants anyway? You see what I did. I what-iffed the trouble.

Now let's say my trouble is that I am too short. Everyone is taller than I am. That's not a lot of trouble. But what if my dream is to star on the basketball team? Now being too short seems more important. I ratcheted up the tension by making the dream more difficult to obtain. I created more of an obstacle.

The obstacle is what stands between a character's trouble and his or her dream. *Trouble > Obstacle Wall < Dream*

Hollywood producers say that a good obstacle is what makes or breaks a screenplay. Think of any movie and ask your students what the obstacle is.

> *Example:* **Finding Nemo**
>
> **Dream:**   To get back home
>
> **Obstacle:** The ocean; ending up in a fish tank

The third act of the movie is devoted to how Nemo overcomes the obstacle, with a little help from his friends in the dentist's office fish tank. When characters need to overcome something, a story has movement and interest.

With a partner, try "what-iffing" your character's trouble, his or her dream, and the obstacle of your story.

Debriefing

What happened when you what-iffed your character's trouble? What happened when you what-iffed their dream? Could you what-if your character's obstacle? What makes a character interesting to a reader? What makes a character interesting to you?

TRY THIS!

THE THREE-ACT STORY

All Hollywood movies follow the same three-act story formula, so they serve as great models for students, especially those students who do not read regularly. But this lesson is not about dumbing-down stories. The three-act formula is actually a great jumping-off point for creating an interesting story. Think of a story as an atom. All atoms have a nucleus, protons, and electrons, but they are not all the same. Even the most complex and individual story is built on the solid foundation of the three-act story. Here's how to teach it.

Model It

1. Talk to your students about what makes a good story. Tell them that all stories have three acts. The first act is the setup. This is where the author sets up the character's trouble. The second act is the mix-up. This is where the character faces various obstacles. In Act 3, the story is resolved in some way.
   Let's take a classic children's story like "Goldilocks and the Three Bears":

   Act 1: Goldilocks has run away. She is alone, hungry, cold, and tired. That's her trouble. She sees a little cottage and goes to investigate.

   Act 2: She tries the right porridge, the right chair, and finally, the right bed to sleep in. End of Act 2.

   Act 3: The Bears come home, surprise the sleeping Goldie, and she runs away. The story is resolved.

   Point out to the students how this particular children's story builds a lot of suspense. If the bears come home too early, we lose the second act and move too quickly to the resolution. Have you ever written or read a story that did this?
   If you go to a movie theater and set your watch alarm for 29 minutes you will find that the first act of most movies ends after almost exactly 29

minutes. The second act takes up most of the movie, and Act 3 often starts when there are 29 minutes left until the end of the film.

One idea to try is to bring in some DVDs of popular movies and watch the first 29 minutes of each one. Stop the movie at these places and ask the students to define the character's trouble and the character's dream. Biopics work especially well because everyone knows the end of the movie without watching it. For example, in *Walk the Line*, a movie about the life of Johnny Cash, Act 1 ends with his audition in Sam Phillips' Sun Studio. The session is going really badly until Sam asks Johnny if he has anything else to sing besides the boring old gospel songs he has chosen. Johnny starts to sing a halting version of "Folsom Prison Blues," and we hear his voice emerging for the first time. At that point in the movie, we know that, as a young boy, his older brother was killed in a sawmill accident and that Johnny felt responsible. We know that Johnny's dad never forgave him for his brother's death and that Johnny joined the Air Force to escape his painful childhood. Twenty-nine minutes into the movie we hear Johnny Cash begin to funnel his trouble into a song, and the first act is complete.

2. Now make a copy of the form on page 233 or create your own three-act story form. Each act should have an obstacle running through it. Obstacles often change as a story progresses. In *Finding Nemo*, the obstacle in Act 2 is surviving the dangers of the deep. In Act 3, the obstacle is getting out of a fish tank.

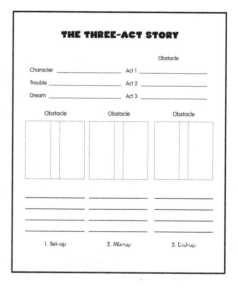

3. Fill in the form with a story about the character you have created. Don't worry if you can't think of everything that happens in the story. What is the trouble in Act 1? What is the trouble in Act 2? How might the trouble resolved in Act 3?

4. Share your story ideas with the class. Try what-iffing the trouble, the dream, and the plot of the story.

5. Try writing the story, but don't use your three-act form as an outline to follow. Rather, just remember it and realize you can what-if the elements of a story at any stage in the process. Begin your story close to your character's trouble. Start at a place of interest or drama and let the story flow from that moment.

Debriefing

Was it easy to plan Act 1 of the story now that you know about your character's trouble? Did the obstacle change or stay the same? Can you "what-if" the obstacle in Act 2 and Act 3 to ratchet up the tension in the story? Does your character's dream pull him or her through the story or is a bigger dream required? What makes your character interesting?

ONCE UPON A TIME THERE WAS A CELL PHONE . . .

Learning Nonfiction Storytelling from Steve Jobs

In his groundbreaking book, *A Whole New Mind*, author Daniel Pink calls storytelling one of the six key skills Americans need to be successful in the crowded 21st-century global marketplace. Many products look the same, taste the same, and smell the same, so if you design something unique, you need to give it a reason that will enable consumers to understand its uniqueness. You can't just sell it with boring accolades the way so many products have been sold over the years. You need a story.

On January 9, 2007, Steve Jobs, the legendary CEO of Apple, stands on the stage at Macworld in his trademark black turtleneck and blue jeans. Here's what he does not say, "Apple has made this really cool new product that combines Web browser, iPod, navigator, and cell phone. It's called the iPhone and you will be amazed at how revolutionary it is."

Instead, Steve Jobs tells a story, and like the best storytellers, he doles out just enough information to hold the interest of the audience. The main character of this story is Mr. Smartphone. His trouble is that he is boring. He has plastic keys that are hard to operate, and he is rigid and unable to adapt to future ideas. It was in some ways the same problem Apple had solved by introducing the user interface and mouse to the boring personal computer way back in the early 80s.

After a more in-depth discussion of what is wrong with cell phones, Jobs then introduced a phone without plastic keys, just a slab of glass and your finger as the pointing device: the iPhone.

When Steve Jobs got to the end of his short speech, Apple stock shot up 10 points. Two months later, more than 11,000 articles had been written about the iPhone before anyone had even held one. Steve Jobs is some storyteller, and we can teach our students to use the same narrative techniques to draw in readers, no matter what subject they are writing about.

TRY THIS!

THE THREE-ACT DOCUMENTARY: USING STICKY-NOTES TO TELL THE STORY

Now let's take what we know about story and character and apply it to persuasive nonfiction writing. Here are two of the most influential documentaries of recent years, *An Inconvenient Truth* by Al Gore, and *Sicko* by Michael Moore. Both point out serious trouble in the world and suggest a path for change. Gore's film is about waking up to the problems of global warming and Moore's film is about fixing problems with America's health-care system.

Model It

Watch one or both movies with your class and have your students think about how the subject of the film might be considered the main character. In other words, if the health-care system is the character of Moore's film, what is its trouble, and what is its dream? What are the obstacles? Fill out the three-act story form for this documentary.

Do It

Create your own outline for a documentary film using the three-act formula. Imagine interviews you could do or places you could travel. Use Post-its to write down interviews or facts and decide in which act of the story to place them.

Example:

Act 1: The rainforests are being destroyed. This will lead to more CO_2 in the atmosphere.

Act 2: Scientists are trying to convince businesspeople to do something about it.

Act 3: What you can do to solve the problem

Debriefing

Was it easy to fill out the form? What are the similarities between a fictional story and a nonfiction story? How does a nonfiction filmmaker illustrate obstacles? What were the challenges in outlining your documentary? What makes a documentary interesting?

THE THREE PRINCES

When my oldest daughter, Jessie, was a little girl, I used to tell her "three prince stories" late at night. The three princes wanted to rescue a princess but each lacked certain essential qualities. The first prince was smart but not brave or kind. The second prince was brave but not smart or kind. The third prince was kind but not brave or smart, and he had a habit of fainting. On their own, none would be capable of rescuing a princess, but together they had a shot. In the story, the obstacles were dragons, moats, wizards, goblins, and secret passageways that lead them astray. I was a young, weary parent, and some nights I would try to get to the end of the story quickly so I could go to bed myself. When I did this, Jessie would scold me:

"Dad, you didn't put enough stuff in the story."

"What do you mean, *stuff*?"

"You got to the end too quick."

Sometimes she would tell me to stop and she would start telling the story, adding more obstacles and plot points herself. It was clear that she knew what made a story tick, even at the tender age of 5. She also knew that good stories could keep you up late, even on school nights.

School systems often downplay the importance of story. Students write them in elementary school but then, as they go up the grades, story writing is replaced by other types writing. Daniel Pink would say that these schools rob students of the most valuable writing skill for the 21st century. Let me put it another way:

> ### LANE'S THIRD LAW OF STORIES
>
> All writing, no matter what genre, is a story.
> If you don't want to know what happens next, it's not worth reading.

Teach your students to see that the elements of a good story are the elements of good writing in any genre. Trouble and dreams, problems and goals fuel all writing.

"YEAH, BUT . . ."
Readers' Questions Answered

How do you deal with kids who just want to write about superheroes and cartoon characters or video games?

In his book *Everything Bad for You Is Good for You*, Steven Johnson points out some of the higher-order thinking skills that many video games promote. For example, a game like *The Sims* is unlike any game I played as a kid because there are no winners and no losers. The game encourages playful, creative character development, architectural finesse, and interpersonal know-how. The more you play the game, the more intricate the world you create. It is important to be familiar with the world of video games so you can understand how many of your students think about stories. For example, video games rarely end; they are like a story with many episodes. One lesson is to show students what makes a superhero interesting. They need obstacles. Superman without kryptonite is just another mighty being. The same ideas that apply to characters apply to superheroes.

What if kids create a very silly character and a very silly story? Isn't this counterproductive?

No. In fact, a very silly cartoon character is a great way to experiment with the concepts learned in this chapter. His silliness makes it easier to make his story miserable and/or triumphant.

You seem to be saying that there is no difference between nonfiction writing and fiction writing. There is. I teach high school and we must teach students about academic writing to prepare them for college. Mustn't we?

Okay. You got me. I understand the importance of what is sometimes referred to as formal academic writing, but I also know that the best academic writing has a voice behind it. Not an informal voice ("Hi, my name is Bill and I'm going to tell you about protozoa . . .") but a creative, inquisitive voice that makes you want to keep flipping the pages. In Malcolm Gladwell's *Blink* and *The Tipping Point*, both of which deal with hard science, Gladwell seduces his readers into his investigation and delights them with the facts he uncovers. Any kid who can write like that in college will rake in the As, and if he or she writes a Ph.D. dissertation, it might get published without major rewriting.

What do you do with kids who just won't end a story? They just keep going on and on and on.

This is more of a problem since the advent of video games that do tend to go on and on. Mini-lessons on endings can help enormously. In my book *Reviser's Toolbox*, I talk about defining different types of endings with your students. These include the loop ending, the surprise ending, and the mysterious ending. Find individual examples of these kinds of endings in books, poems, or even movies, then encourage your students to try using one in their own writing. I also recommend the book *Mentor Texts* by Lynne R. Dorfman and Rose Cappelli and *Cracking Open the Author's Craft* by Lester Laminack for more ideas about crafting endings.

CHAPTER 7

GENRE, GENDER, AND JE NE SAIS QUOI

Creating Writing Assignments That Last Forever

This is my childhood friend Paul Topham with his favorite teacher, Mrs. Bloom, from second grade. Paul was the class clown and was known to teachers as a difficult child. He logged more time in the principal's office than probably any student in the Dover, New Hampshire, school system. In fact, years after high school, when Paul had a job working for the state that required a visit to his alma mater, the old principal, Harvey Knepp, issued an urgent warning over the loudspeaker. "Warning: Paul Topham is in the building! Paul Topham is in the building!" Today Paul is a successful IT director for Timberland shoe company. We honored his teacher, Mrs. Bloom, a few years ago with the very first Miss Foley Award. (You can nominate your own teacher for the award by visiting the teacher center at www.discoverwriting.com.) We chose Mrs. Bloom for a number of reasons. The most compelling was simple: Across his 12 years of schooling, she was Paul Topham's favorite teacher. "What did Mrs. Bloom do?" I asked Paul.

> The pen is the tongue of the mind.
>
> —*Miguel de Cervantes*

Paul Topham with Mrs. Bloom

"We did workbooks until 10 a.m. each day and then went to play centers for the rest of the day," Paul said. Paul had figured out that Mrs. Bloom always started checking workbooks in the front of the room and never reached his seat in the back. Therefore, he would not do his workbook but just wait until play center time. Then one day she started in the back and Paul was caught. Even so, Paul was delighted when Mrs. Bloom found him out because she was one of the few teachers who truly understood and appreciated him. The other reason Paul loved her is that Mrs. Bloom knew that learning had to be enjoyable to be memorable. I knew this too because my older brother Michael repeated second grade because he could not read. The school placed him in Mrs. Bloom's class and he was reading within a month. Mrs. Bloom's secret: She let him read his favorite, Superman comics, in class.

At Miss Foley Day, at which I presented the award, Paul sat in the second row behind Mrs. Bloom, who is now in her 80s. There was one moment when I was describing the play centers in her second-grade classroom (a sort of Montessori program built into a traditional 1950s classroom) and Mrs. Bloom turned around and put her hand on Paul's hand and said, "We had fun, didn't we?"

It was a moment I will remember forever because, for me, it touched on what teaching is about: the bond, the relationship between teacher and student, and how it endures across the decades. When I looked at the grown-up Paul Topham and the old but radiant Mrs. Bloom holding his hand, a variation on a classic movie phrase came to mind: "We'll always have second grade."

In this chapter I want to show you how your writing program can help you reach offbeat students like Paul with assignments and extraordinary opportunities that go outside the little box we call school and endure through the ages.

BEYOND QUIZZES AND BOOK REPORTS

A while back, I wrote a book titled *51 Wacky We-search Reports* for students like Paul Topham. The book demonstrates how to create research paper assignments that bring out the inner voice and humor in students while exploring different learning styles. Teachers can use these funny assignments to supplement or replace boring school assignments like quizzes or tests, which research shows don't really help students to remember material past the day of the test.

Here is one wacky we-search report, called a "How-To" poem. In *A Whole New Mind*, Daniel Pink calls "symphony" an essential skill for Americans to learn in the 21st century. Symphony is the ability to make connections, to take in disparate bits of information and synthesize them so the big picture emerges. "How-To" poems teach symphony to your students.

Upgrading Our Sense of Humor

If the students are having a good time, can they be learning? The answer is a resounding (if I may misquote Molly Bloom) "Yes, Yes, Oh, yes!"

Gilda Radner said, "Humor is truth, only quicker." Charlie Chaplin said, "Humor heightens our sense of survival and preserves our sanity." Steve Martin said, "A joke that works is complete knowledge in a nanosecond." All these people grasped something that our public school system has yet to understand. Humor is a learning tool of the highest magnitude. If you can harness it as a teacher, you have split the atom. Your class will never run out of energy.

Silly Is Silly but Funny Is True

One problem is that some teachers think that all humor is silly. Not true. Silly is just silly, but funny is true. Have you ever laughed when you should not have been laughing? In church perhaps, or at a funeral or a staff meeting? Your friend turns to you and asks, "Why are you laughing?" You heave sighs, your face turns red. "I don't know," you say.

One way to teach this is to make a silly school rule: "All students will run in the halls at all times." To make this silly rule funny, I need a rationale that's true and specific. Example: "Students will arrive in class more quickly, ready to collapse in their chairs and sit still." We laugh at shared truth. In school we have a word for specific shared truths. We call them facts. The more specific facts you can put into a wacky we-search paper, the funnier it gets and the less silly it is. If you have students in your class who are more interested in good laughs than getting good grades, wacky we-search is for them.

Never start a wacky we-search assignment without having serious facts and "ooh!" facts on the table.

But I'm Not a Funny Person, How Can I Possibly Teach Humor?

This is a line I hear often from teachers across the country. The answer is you don't have to be the funny person; you can be the straight man, like Seinfeld, who surrounded himself with funny actors and just reacted to them. Your students can get all the laughs. Let me introduce you to your new friends, Mr. Setup and Mr. Punch. Mr. Setup is the guy with the tie, and Mr. Punch is the guy with the pie. Mr. Setup, on his own, is just a boring guy with a tie and Mr. Punch, on his own, is just a silly guy standing around with a pie. But put the two together and you get humor.

Mr. Setup and Mr. Punch

Copyright ©2003 from *51 Wacky We-search Reports*

TRY THIS!

WACKY WE-SEARCH 101: STRAY THOUGHTS AND BIOGRAPHY BUBBLES

Here is a way to teach Mr. Setup and Mr. Punch to your students. This relationship is the foundation of a successful wacky we-search paper.

Model It

Tell your students that the funniest humor mixes serious facts with funny stuff. Explain that one way to plan a report is to divide a sheet of paper into two columns. One side is for the setup—all the serious facts you have gathered. The second side is for the silly stuff, the "ooh!" facts, and anything else that may or may not be true.

Example: **George Washington**

Setup	Punch
He refused to be king. He was a Federalist and a surveyor.	He had wooden teeth. He was married to Martha. He was tall. He didn't tell lies. He cut down a cherry tree.

Next, put a picture of your person on a blank page and put thought bubbles over his or her head. Add some serious facts mixed with funny ideas. You've created a wacky we-search paper like the one at right.

Debriefing

Were your biography bubbles funny? Which bubbles were the funniest? What did your research reveal to you about your subject? How is doing this different from writing a paper about the person?

For Those Who Can't Sit Still

Another breed of wacky we-search paper involves kinesthetic learning. Close your eyes. Can you think of a student in your class who can't sit still? Chances are, 20 students just raced through your brain. One of them might have looked like a childhood photo of the woman in the photo at right. Her name is Carol Glynn, and I met her years ago at an in-service day in Connecticut.

Based on her own experiences as a child, Carol wrote a book called *Learning on Their Feet: A Sourcebook for Kinesthetic Learning Across the Curriculum K–8*. She travels around the country showing teachers how to get kids learning through movement. One of my favorite wacky we-search papers came from Carol.

Carol Glynn

TRY THIS!

STRUTTING YOUR STUFF

Here we get to create a fashion runway and plug our research into a fashion show.

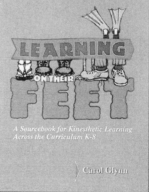

Model It

Talk to your students about fashion shows. Most fashion shows sell clothes, but your fashion show is going to sell your research. To make a really funny fashion show you need to know the two main texts: the text of the body language, and the text of the words.

1. Create a runway in the classroom and ask for volunteers to practice being fashion models. With young students, explain that while it's called a runway, they don't need to run. Practice the walk, the turn, and most importantly, the look. Fashion models never smile. They stare through you.

2. Next talk about the language of fashion shows. On the board, create a list of different parts of speech and the corresponding "language of fashion."

   Nouns

   - Gown
   - Capris
   - Pumps
   - Tops
   - Shawls

   Adjectives

   - Elegant
   - Exquisite
   - Sultry
   - Fashion-forward
   - Wild

   Verbs (Models never simply wear dresses. They . . .)

   - Don
   - Sport
   - Are draped in
   - Are engulfed in
   - Appear in

Do It

Now you are ready to create your fashion show based on whatever content you are studying. Pick music to go along with the narration. Decide how the models will walk to portray your subject. If you have time, create costumes and invite parents in to see the fashion show.

Here's one idea for doing a fashion show while teaching geology and/or history. (You can see a nine-minute video of Carol Glynn doing a fashion show at www.discoverwriting.com.)

The Rock Fashion Show

And now, direct from northern Italy and central Vermont, we have Marble. Sporting a calcite and dolomite crystal ensemble designed by Metamorphosis, the famous Greek designer, this marble carries a sleek limestone finish. Its stylish snow white color can fool you at first, because if you look closely, across the shoulders, you'll glimpse tints of red, yellow, pink, and green caused by impurities in the stone that actually add to its chic beauty. Marble is often used to create statues and the columns of classical buildings. So don't expect her to hang out in your neighborhood unless you're friends with the gods. Thank you, Marble.

Copyright ©2003 from 51 Wacky We-search Reports

Debriefing

What was the funniest thing in your fashion show? What was the silliest thing? Did using more real facts make it funnier? What could you do to make your fashion show better? Can you see that the more truthful your fashion show is, the funnier it is?

Deconstructing Voice

Wacky we-search stimulates writing voices. I have developed a workshop called "Voice Lessons in Nonfiction Writing." On the next page is an acrostic I created to show teachers how to create conditions for students to develop their voices as writers.

Looking at this brief definition, it's clear that wacky we-search addresses all these letters and helps build voice in content-area and writing classrooms. Yet assignments like this are not the norm in American classrooms. Indeed, whenever authorities criticize the public school system, you rarely hear them denouncing the lack of creativity. Rather, they long for stricter standards and more testing, which promotes even more rigid cookie-cutter instruction.

Ironically, business gurus like Tom Peters say that America's main edge in the global economy is the ability of the typical American to think outside the box. Countries like India, China, and Japan have highly skilled labor forces willing to work for very little money, but these countries don't have the creative spark and the symphonic minds to design the original products the world wants.

> ### What Is Voice?
>
> **V is for Visualize Audience.** Students who write with voice aren't writing for a teacher or an assignment but for a real audience.
>
> **O is for Organize Outside the Box.** Students who write with voice organize their writing around their own curiosity (see Chapter 4).
>
> **I is for Interpret From the Inside Out.** Students who write with voice don't hold their subject at a distance. They get inside their topic.
>
> **C is for Craft Choices.** Students who write with voice know there are many ways to write a paragraph. They understand craft.
>
> **E is for Elaboration.** Students who write with voice know how to find the details that really bring home their message.

We need a public school system that nurtures our creative voices and dares students to take risks, that celebrates real learning, not a system that tries to eliminate diversity and creativity in favor of uniform standards.

Until then, it's probably important in some schools that you don't tell your principal you are doing wacky we-search. Tell him instead you are simply doing "multi-genre" work. He will understand that.

Boy Crisis Solved: Let Them Write About the World They Live In

Recently there have been a lot of books about the boy crisis in education. Research shows that in the area of literacy, boys are much less likely to be readers by the time they are out of high school. In his groundbreaking book, *Misreading Masculinity: Boys, Literacy, and Popular Culture*, Thomas Newkirk says a prejudice exists among many public school teachers in favor of certain approved genres, such as memoir, fiction, report writing, the five-paragraph theme, the persuasive essay, and the research paper. The boys who write about video games, comic books, movie previews, or comedy are shunned or told to do this kind of writing on their own time. Consequently, boys don't always see the relevance of school to things that really interest them.

Newkirk recommends that teachers give boys more latitude to explore genres from popular culture. It is important that teachers meet them halfway and not impose an arbitrary standard. I encourage teachers to seek out new genres every waking hour and introduce them to their writing workshop. Here is an example of a wacky we-search report that fits the bill.

TRY THIS!

THE 30-SECOND TEASER SPOT

How many movie previews (also known as trailers) do you think your students have seen by the time they reach high school? A minimum of several thousand, one would think. So here is a structure that they know by heart, and yet how many teachers have ever considered having their students try writing movie previews?

Model It

Show a few movie previews to your class. You can download many online by going to Web sites like Apple (www.apple.com/trailers). You can also just bring in a DVD or videocassette and watch the trailers that come with the film.

1. Watch a preview all the way through. Talk to your students about what makes a preview effective.

   - It shows you small parts of the movie.

   - It creates a quick version of the movie.

   - Sometimes they come up with a little catchphrase or slogan for the movie. For example, "I see dead people."

2. Watch the same preview without sound and snap your fingers or have your students clap their hands when each shot ends. It's usually every two seconds.

3. Ask student to write a short preview of a movie about something you are studying in science, math, or social studies.

4. *Optional*: Write your own preview (see illustration, next page) and share with the class.

   Example:

   She was a North American continent warmed by the summer sun.

   He was a current somewhere in the Pacific.

   Alone, they lived separate but peaceful lives.

   Until one fall, he came to visit!

   Coming this November to a theater near you.

   EL NINO!

   Rated: BU (Bring Umbrella)

Writing a movie preview teaches the skill of summarization, but it is much different than the kinds of summaries students are used to because they get to put their own spin on the main points. It's fun, and they can even act it out with their friends.

TRY THIS!

LETTER HOME TO PARENTS

Writing a parody of "school-sanctioned genres," like the research report, is also a great way to hook boys into writing. Newkirk's research shows that young boys have a much higher interest in parody than girls, but schools don't always appreciate or encourage parody assignments.

You can also try an excuse letter from home about why a certain homework assignment didn't get done. Frank McCourt wrote a lovely story about inventing this genre in his best-selling book *Teacher Man*.

Copyright ©2003 from 51 Wacky We-search Reports

Model It

1. Ask your students if they have ever had a letter sent home about something they did in school. If they can find such a letter, have them share it with the class, or better yet, write one with the students.

2. Ask your students to write a letter home to parents reporting misbehavior that relates to the subject you're studying. Tell them to draw upon interesting facts about the subject in their letters.

Dear Comma Mama,

I regret to inform you that your son has been causing excessive pauses within our sentences. He has been cavorting with the conjunctions And, Or, But, nor and others while not working independently. We expect him to break up the naughty nouns and flirty phrases when they appear in groups of three or more, but he has neglected his duty! He has also been caught running between independent clauses without any support. Please respond immediately to this situation, and by all means make sure to put it in the correct place so as to not cause us unnecessary pause!

Sincerely,
Principal Punctuation

What Do Girls Need?

If boys need more leeway to explore genres from popular culture, girls need a chance to examine cultural norms and beliefs that have historically kept women down.

When my daughter Jessie was in sixth grade, she met with a group of four girls once a week to discuss women's issues. The program was funded by a grant and it was called "Girls Speak Out." They talked about women's movements around the world and saw footage from the Fourth World Conference on Women, September 14–15, 1995, in Beijing. Jessie is now in her early 20s, and she looks back on those brief meetings as the first time she saw herself as a woman. At the time, the program was controversial. The all-male school board in our small Vermont town said we needed to also have a "Boys Speak Out" program to make it equal. At a meeting, I joked, "We already do have a 'Boys Speak Out' program. We call it the school board." (No one laughed.)

My comment may not be that far from the truth. Girls need time to create an identity in a world that even today, though arguably to a lesser extent, is still run by men. When a young mother named Elizabeth Cady Stanton moved from Boston to Seneca Falls, New York, in 1848 she felt a sense of social isolation similar to what my sixth-grade daughter felt in our tiny rural town in Vermont. Stanton lived in a man's world and had no voice in that world. The Seneca Falls conference was the first "girls speak out" conference on the planet. And the women's movement is today far from over. Women are still paid less for the same job. Clearly, they have not yet achieved equality, but as long as young women are aware, there is hope for continued progress. That's where teachers come in.

Here is one of my favorite ways to introduce a writing assignment on gender equity. Read it aloud or give copies to your students.

TRY THIS!

GENDER BENDING

The Barbie Liberation Front

Imagine the Barbie Liberation Front, a group of activists who buy Barbies and G.I. Joes, take them home, and switch the voice chips. Then, they return the dolls to the stores in unopened boxes. Picture a little girl as she pushes the button on Malibu Barbie, and she barks out, "Vengeance is mine." Picture a little boy opening up his G.I. Joe and hearing, "Let's go to the mall!" Playing with gender expectations is a great way to use writing to uncover stereotypes masquerading as truth.

Model It

Talk with your students about what it is like growing up as a boy or a girl. What is their earliest memory of their gender? If you can, show a tape of commercials for toys meant for boys and toys that target girls.

Older students might be interested in a 1966 definition of "woman," taken from a popular encyclopedia. Have them write a response.

It begins, "There are important differences between men and women beyond the primary fact that women are the mothers of men." As it progresses, it gets condescending. "Men in general are stronger and quicker than women, although there are many exceptions to this rule. A champion woman tennis player can defeat thousands of ordinary men players, for example."

Do It

Ask your students to bring in ads and photos from fashion magazines showing men and women. Pin them up on a bulletin board. Ask three students of the same gender to come up to the front of the room. Ask them to choose one picture with a person of the opposite gender and stare at it for a while, noticing the details of the model's pose. Then, have students turn and face the class and hold the model's pose for five seconds without giggling. It's really hard to do, and I guarantee your students will love it if you model it for them. What do the poses say about men and women?

Discuss the stereotypes that are used to define boys and girls. Write about how you fit or don't fit the stereotype of a boy or girl. Experiment with writing in an exaggerated male or female voice.

Debriefing

What is a stereotype? How does is it differ from a real person? Why do people create stereotypes? Have you ever been stereotyped? How do we resist stereotypes?

TRY THIS!

MARLBORO MAN AND VIRGINIA SLIMS WOMAN

Cigarette ads have exploited gender stereotypes for years. Two of the most successful campaigns in the history of advertising have been the Marlboro Man and the Virginia Slims woman. The former tapped into a man's need to feel macho in an increasingly less macho world, and the latter connected cigarette smoking with the women's liberation movement of the late 1960s. The lung cancer rate among women tripled from the 1960s to the '90s, due in part to Virginia Slims. Research shows that most smokers for life have puffed a cigarette by the age of 11. Here is a way for students to separate the stereotype from the reality. The true account of the Marlboro Man can be found at http://www.worldsfastestclown.com/man_dies.html.

*Me revising the slogan of a Marlboro billboard to read "Come to where the **cancer** is."*

Model It

Bring in magazine ads of the Marlboro man and Virginia Slims woman. In Canada, magazine ads for cigarettes have been banned for years, but they are still plentiful in the U.S. Show the ads to your students. Talk about what the message is and who the audience is. Here is a question list for analyzing ads.

Analyzing Advertisements

- Who is the audience?
- What is the message?
- What is the truth about the product?
- What is the not-so-true image?

Do It

1. Ask two girls and two boys to come up to the front of the class and study the body language and the look of the Marlboro man and the Virginia Slims woman. Tell the students they are going to have a rare opportunity. They are going to get a chance to interview the Marlboro man or the Virginia Slims woman. They are going to speak with a genuine stereotypical image.

   One at a time, have them turn around and transform into the Marlboro man or Virginia Slims woman. Give them a pen to act as their cigarette (the kids love that part) and have them role-play the part as the class asks questions. Make sure the kids ask the tough questions, such as, "If you know that smoking is bad for you, why do you still do it?" "Would you want your children to smoke?" Typically, the images respond glibly.

   - Why do you smoke? *It makes me look cool.*

   - Don't you know you are going to die? *We all die.*

   - But you are dying sooner. *But I look cool, don't I?*

   - Do you want your children to smoke? *Sure, as long as they don't take mine.*

2. Ask your Marlboro man and Virginia Slims woman to take their bows and go back to their seats. Discuss the experience. What did we learn about stereotypes? Are they real people? What makes them images?

3. Ask students to write about the difference between an image and a real person.

Debriefing

What is the main difference between an image and a person? Have you ever felt that you were expected to act like an image and not a person? How does knowing about stereotypes help a person live in today's world?

CRANBERRY RELISH DAY

Miss Whiting was my fifth-grade teacher. She was an older woman with white curly hair that appeared to be in a hairnet even though it wasn't. She grew up in the days when women sometimes went into teaching for all the wrong reasons.

Namely, they didn't want to be a nurses, housewives, or librarians. She screamed at her class, an awful high-pitched scream that would peel the paint off the walls and echo across the playground.

She always wore the same dark blue polka-dotted dresses, and because of her weak knees, she wrapped ace bandages around them that sometimes dangled beneath the hem of her dress. Everything she taught was out of the book and worksheets. Her spelling books could give you asthma; they were originally blue, but time and mildew had turned them a shade of green. Her assignments were so boring and routine it was hard to stay awake in her class, and she often chided students for what she called "woolgathering," Miss Whiting's term for staring out the window and trying to think of something interesting. She also picked a few favorite students and held them up as good examples while the rest of us just sat there in our straight rows, neglected, bored, and wishing we were somewhere else.

But once a year, Miss Whiting's students made cranberry relish. "Oh yes, we must not forget Cranberry Relish Day, children!" she would say. "Do your homework or you may not be allowed to participate in Cranberry Relish Day." All September long she would goad us on with the promise of the glorious Cranberry Relish Day. This was the day when there would be no quizzes, no homework assignments to complete, no insidious fill-in-the-blank workbook units to finish. This was Cranberry Relish Day.

And at last, some time in mid-November, before Thanksgiving, the sacred day would arrive, and we would show up at school with our pound of cranberries, our sugar, and our apples. You didn't want to be sick that day. And at the front of the room was Miss Whiting's desk, bare except for two hot plates. And all day long, as promised, we made cranberry relish (actually, only her three favorite students would make it—we just sat at our desks and watched, but it was still exciting). And when we walked home from school that day, we each carried a pint ball jar of relish for Thanksgiving dinner.

After that day and all year long, Miss Whiting would talk about Cranberry Relish Day. "These worksheets are pretty boring, children, but remember, we did make cranberry relish! Didn't we? Back in November. Remember?"

Years later, as luck would have it, my parents bought a house on the same dead-end street as Miss Whiting. She had long since retired from teaching, and she lived alone with a tiny pug that she walked religiously morning and night. I would sometimes speak with her and tell her what I was doing now. She seemed very lonely and sad now that she was away from the school, and she lavished all her attention on that yippy little pug, who would charge anyone who came near her.

Once she asked me what I remembered from her classroom. I paused for a moment and could see a remoteness cloud her eyes, a remoteness I would remember a few years later when I heard of her suicide. What else was there for me to say?

"Cranberry Relish Day."

"Of course," she said, a smile gracing her lips. "Cranberry Relish Day. You know, for 30 years, every November, we made cranberry relish."

"I know," I said, suddenly feeling a surprising compassion for the woman who had so tormented my fifth-grade year.

"We loved Cranberry Relish Day."

Let's make more cranberry relish in school. Let's give assignments and create opportunities for learning that students remember long after they leave school. I hope this chapter inspires you to create assignments that step outside the box we call school so you can reach out to your students and introduce them to a larger world.

"YEAH, BUT . . ."
Readers' Questions Answered

If I let boys write whatever they want, they might write violent stuff. I don't want to read that or encourage it. What do I do?

Teachers have good reasons for banning certain writing genres from their classrooms. Since the school shootings in Columbine and at Virginia Tech, teachers are increasingly aware of their responsibility to safeguard their learning environments.

You can make guidelines and set standards about violence and writing, but always be willing to break them if they get in the way of what you see as meaningful expression. In his book *Boy Writers*, Ralph Fletcher recommends treating issues of violence in writing on a case-by-case basis and not making too many rigid general rules that might limit a boy's range of expression. In *Misreading Masculinity*, Thomas Newkirk argues that when boys are shooting for violence they are often looking for humor and missing wildly. Showing them how to write funny can be the ticket to solving the problem. Study a model author like Dav Pilkey and his Captain Underpants books and see how he uses humor effectively. Newkirk has also found in his interviews with boy writers that when they are allowed to write about violence, they develop a subtle sense of what violence is necessary and what is gratuitous. They learn to interpret the violence around them.

My kids get uncomfortable when I bring up issues like gender roles. Isn't it a parent's job to educate kids about stuff like this? And besides, I have barely enough time to teach the academic material. Am I now supposed to teach them a social curriculum as well? Is it really all that necessary?

Of course, you have to teach inside your own comfort zone, but maybe that zone itself is the problem. It is uncomfortable to critically examine gender roles. Your boys might find they hold prejudiced views toward girls, and vice versa. We never had opportunities to explore gender when I was in school. In today's world, students should understand both the legal and moral ramifications of such challenges as sexual harassment, before they hit the workplace.

Movie previews and other wacky we-searches look like fun, but students are really learning. Very few of our students are going to be movie producers when they grow up, but many more will have to write *real* research papers in college and reports in the real world. Are "fun" assignments really justifiable, considering the curriculum demands placed upon us?

Dr. Darla Shaw, a professor at Western Connecticut State University, found that just one wacky we-search paper assignment addressed between 25 and 30 of the state's performance standards. Not only that, the graduate students found the assignments to be enjoyable. In their closing essays, they said that doing wacky we-search was the most engaging assignment they had done in six years of college. Though students might not do many wacky we-search papers in life, the thinking and writing skills they learn as a result prepare them for success in the 21st century.

CHAPTER 8

LITERACY WITHOUT BOUNDARIES

In 2007, the International Reading Association met in Toronto, Ontario, for its yearly meeting. Because new rules require passports for travel to Canada, and U.S. school districts refuse to pay teachers for foreign travel expenses, only 6,000 teachers showed up to an event that typically draws 20,000. Ironically, the theme of the conference was "Literacy Without Boundaries."

> Write what should not be forgotten . . .
>
> —*Isabel Allende*

One of my main reasons for fleeing our safe nation and

Iqbal Masih

journeying to the exotic international capitol of Toronto was to hear the founder of Free the Children, Craig Kielburger, speak. I learned about Craig years ago through my friend Ann Barnett, a teacher from Houston, Texas, whose middle school students had built a school in Ecuador through Free the Children. As an 11-year-old, Craig had read about a boy, a Pakistani carpet weaver named Iqbal Masih, who at the tender age of six was sold by his parents to a carpet maker and chained to a loom where for the next six years he wove carpets seven days a week, 16 hours a day.

Because of their small fingers, children are sought after as carpet weavers, and though this form of bonded slavery has been outlawed by the Pakistani courts, the practice persists in a country where illiteracy rates allow unscrupulous businessmen to make up their own laws.

Iqbal Masih refused to be a slave. As a 12-year-old, he formed a union among the carpet weavers and became an advocate for the abolishment of child labor. He was awarded Reebok's Human Rights Youth Action Award in 1994, but soon after he returned to Pakistan, he was murdered. When the press asked his sister to comment on her brother's death, she said, "You can kill one Iqbal, but the moment you do, 1,000 new ones get born."

Many thousands of miles away in Toronto, Canada, a middle school student named Craig Kielburger carried a small newspaper clipping in his hands as he walked. He had seen it that morning when his family did its daily ritual of laying the newspaper out on the table at breakfast. Iqbal's death outraged young Craig Kielburger the way only a middle school student, first encountering the injustice of the world, can be outraged. He brought the article to school, showed it to his teacher, and asked, "How can this happen today?" Instead of shrugging his shoulders and saying that's the way the world is, Craig's teacher turned it into a challenge. "What are you going to do about it?" he asked. That day Craig shared the article with the class and said he wanted to start an organization where

Craig Kielburger

children help to get other children out of slavery. The hands of 18 children who wanted to help went up, and Free the Children was born.

Craig's teacher could have easily said, "You know, I'm glad you are a concerned world citizen, but this is school and we have lesson plans and a midterm to prepare for. We can talk about this another time." The world is glad he didn't. So far, Craig's organization has built more than 450 schools and has been nominated for a Nobel Prize three times. Craig Kielburger is 25 years old.

In this chapter we are going to learn a few ways to extend literacy instruction beyond the walls of the classroom and out into the big world. Some of you might be thinking, I don't even have enough time to teach my students and meet standards without adding "save the world" to the list. Well, brain research shows that students will remember what they learn only when teachers make it what education expert Janet Allen calls "M and M": *meaningful and memorable*. Educational standards for the 21st century require students to take a vested interest in their learning. Even assembly-line jobs today require workers to take an active role to improve job performance. The days of punching a clock and waiting for the coffee break buzzer are over, and our classrooms must strive to be more than just holding tanks for society. They must be breeding grounds for meaningful, thoughtful work. They must create learners who can solve problems that have not even occurred yet.

BYTES, BLOGS, AND BEYOND

This is my friend Luis Dechtiar. I have known Luis since he was 14 years old, when he moved to Vermont from Brazil. From the youngest age, Luis has been interested in being a filmmaker and serving the world. He attended Emerson College, studied film, and won several prestigious prizes there. I could tell you

Luis Dechtiar

more about Luis, but I don't have to. You can find out for yourself by visiting luisdechtiar.net, where you can read Luis's blog and find out the latest news, the movies he has been seeing, his views about art and life. You can watch several of his short films, see all the countries in the world he has visited, and view the photos he has taken. You can read screenplays and find links to other filmmakers and friends of Luis. Because of the Internet, Luis Dechtiar is an international personality, a world citizen. Any person on the planet can reach him with just a point and a click.

Luis's blog exemplifies a new model of literacy for the 21st century. Thomas Friedman presents the negative economic aspects of this phenomenon in his book *The World Is Flat.* Routine blue-collar and white-collar jobs are being outsourced to India and other developing countries. Huge companies like Ford and Microsoft are moving entire divisions offshore, where skills are high and labor is cheap. It has become clear that just as the 19th century belonged to Britain and the 20th century belonged to the United States, the 21st century will most likely belong to China and India and other countries rising beyond their third-world status to economic prominence. In this new world, literacy, self-expression, and connection are central skills for Americans struggling to keep a stake in the global economic marketplace.

Literacy skills are becoming inextricably linked with technological know-how. Can anyone who has seen an effective YouTube flick doubt that video editing is an essential literacy skill of the future?

YouTube is the result of three young people who had a vision, captured that vision in words, won the support of venture capitalists, and then worked with software developers and the general public to refine that vision. America's key advantage on the world stage is its ability to imagine extraordinary enterprises like YouTube, Facebook, Yahoo, and Google and bring them into being. Our schools must teach students that literacy is not an end in itself. It can bring to life a larger vision.

TRY THIS!

THE ANALOG BLOG

Every student in your class, whatever the grade level, should have his or her own blog. A blog is like a public digital journal, a way for kids to tell their friends who they are and what they are thinking. A blog is also a place to clip tidbits from all kinds of sources and share them with others. A blog is a place where readers can respond and interact.

If you have regular Internet access at school, creating a blog will be easy. Check out googleblogspot.com. If you are not connected, you can still do what I call an "analog blog." Create all the elements of a blog in a public personal writing journal. Students swap journals to create the interactive element. Use a bulletin board in your classroom for students to post comments and responses to one another. Think of it as a very low-tech blog that can simulate some of the excitement of a real blog.

Model It

Talk to your students about blogs. Depending on the age of your students, they may know far more than you do. What makes an interesting blog? If you were to create a blog, what would the theme of your blog be?

Do It

1. As a homework assignment or in the computer lab, have your students find three blogs and bring printouts of them to class the next day.

2. Students share the theme of each blog and any technical tips and/or advice they glean from the blog.

3. Students can then plan their own blogs. Discuss the images they will include. How will they design the home page? What do they want to tell about themselves in the blog?

4. If you have Internet access, students create their blogs. If not, they can create an analog blog, pasting in news stories and images from magazines. Include

your comments as short, blog-like commentaries. Have students write to one another's blogs.

Debriefing

What was it like making a blog? Did you find a cause to promote on your blog? How did people respond to your blog? How can you make your blog better?

CALL A MINGA IN YOUR CLASS

Blogs and other Internet-based literacy forms are most powerful when they connect the third world with the first world.

In *Me to We* (cowritten with brother Marc), Craig Kielburger tells a story about a service trip to the mountains of Ecuador that went bad. Because of a mule traffic jam, materials to finish the roof of a school did not arrive in time for the crew of two-dozen high school students to complete the project. Devastated to think that their work to finish the school might come to naught, they asked to meet with the elder of the community, an old woman chosen as leader because of her age. It seemed to them that the old woman did not seem to understand the gravity of the situation. She merely took a sip of tea and said, "No problem." Then she walked out into the village and at the top of her lungs yelled, "Tomorrow, there will be a *minga*!"

Craig and his friends thought she may not have understood what they had told her, but trying to be polite, they did not push the question further. They worked hard all day, but went to bed feeling that their whole project had failed. They had one day to do the work and not enough manpower to complete even half of it.

The next morning they awoke to commotion. Hundreds of people had arrived in the village to complete the work. Some had traveled all evening with children on their backs. They brought food and firewood for cooking. They started work immediately and completed the roof before the end of the day.

Later, when the school was completed, Craig and his friends asked the tribal elder, "What's a minga?" She calmly explained, "In our language, a minga is the coming together of people for the betterment of all." Then she paused a moment and asked, "What is the word in your language?" Craig and his friends struggled for a moment. They were struck by the fact that there was no English word, but they wanted to come up with something for such a profound and important phenomenon. Language reflects culture, and in English there are many words for money but apparently none for this. The best they could come up with was this phrase, "A minga is a 'riot for good.'"

This next lesson begins the process of starting a riot for good in your class.

Tracy's Minga

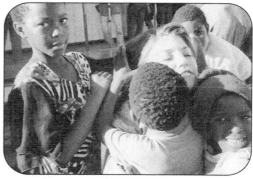

Tracy Kendall with friends in South Africa

In 1994, Tracy Kendall was a spring-semester student teacher when her supervising teacher asked her to create a unit of study on Africa. She designed a unit about South Africa. She wanted her sixth- and seventh-grade students to be able to identify with Africa, so she told them about Amy Biehl, a high school student from Newport, California, who devoted her life to ending the evil system of apartheid after learning of Nelson Mandela's imprisonment.

After showing the video *Amy's Story*, Tracy asked her students two questions.

1. Amy Biehl went halfway around the world to help people she didn't know and it eventually cost her her life. What does that say about Amy's commitment?

2. Is there anything that you could commit to with such dedication?

As with all new lessons, Tracy was not sure how her students would respond. These were kids raised in the suburbs. They hung out at the mall with their friends on weekends. Would they have any interest in helping children in the third world?

When she read their papers she felt the amazement and sweet joy only language arts teachers can feel when an assignment truly hits home. In paper after paper, students wrote about how unfulfilled their lives were, and how they longed to do what Amy Biehl did. Tracy

Amy Biehl with a young girl

wept right there in the classroom, and then she brought the papers home and read them to her mother, and they both wept. Then they got an idea. Let's send the papers to the Biehls so they can see the lasting effect their daughter's all-too-short life had on students halfway across the country, a year and a half after Amy's death. Tracy called the Biehls and left a message asking if they wanted to read what her students had written.

The next day, there was a message on Tracy's answering machine from Peter Biehl. "We are very interested in what your students had to write. Can you call us?" After a 45-minute conversation, Tracy and her father went to meet the Biehls at the second annual Amy Biehl memorial in San Francisco, held at the Great American Music Hall and attended by celebrities such as Danny Glover. A year later, Tracy, her sister Deb, and her parents were in South Africa meeting Nelson Mandela and beginning work with the Amy Biehl Foundation. The following year, they invited me to join them on a trip to South Africa, along with a team of eight teachers from St. Louis.

When Tracy gave that simple assignment to her students, she had no idea it would change her life and the lives of thousands of South African children, but she did know that she cared what her students had to say and wanted them to see they have a great untapped power to change the world. Writing is much more than a tool for communication. It can release a power that connects souls, whether young or old, rich or poor. It connects them with the larger world in ways you cannot even begin to imagine.

TRY THIS!

THE YEARLONG RESEARCH PROJECT

Judy Kendall and Joyce Foster

These are my friends Judy Kendall (Tracy's mom) and Joyce Foster. For over a decade, they have taught what they affectionately call their research project—a yearlong assignment that has students passionately involved in a single subject. Judy and Joyce believe that a student can take a subject and, by adapting it for different audiences, gain a much deeper understanding of it. Also, the process of living with a subject all year long can create a deeper interest that may even last a lifetime. Here is how to begin.

Model It

1. Get passionate. Judy and Joyce believe if students are going to stick with a subject all year long, it better be one they are passionate about. They show their students examples of students who have changed the world.

   Say to your students: Amy Biehl was in high school when she first heard about the apartheid regime in South Africa and the imprisonment of Nelson Mandela. Amy went on to attend Stanford University and became a Fulbright scholar. She traveled to South Africa and helped with the formation of the first post-apartheid government. Tragically, Amy was murdered during racial violence in the Cape Flats town of Guguletu just a few months before the first free election. But even after her death, Amy's work continued. Her parents formed the Amy Biehl Foundation, a nonprofit organization that works to eliminate poverty in the same township where Amy was murdered.

2. Use the newspaper as a menu of choices. In Craig Kielburger's book *Me to We*, Archbishop Desmond Tutu talks about how some people are overwhelmed at the abundance of problems in the world and simply give up trying to solve them. To overcome this feeling of helplessness, he recommends viewing the newspaper as a menu of choices. Bring a newspaper to your class and introduce this concept to your students. Show them a list of causes they can involve themselves with and ask them to choose one.

Do It

1. Ask students to prepare and deliver a short speech. After they have chosen a subject, students engage in preliminary research and present a short speech to the class, highlighting their "ooh!" facts about the subject (see Chapter 3). Follow the speech with a full-class press conference, generating long lists of curious questions for the writer.

2. Have students revise their speeches into short research papers.

3. Have students send their research papers to an expert in the field with a persuasive letter asking them to read it.

4. Have students then write a children's book about their subject for the younger children in the school. They should study nonfiction and fictional children's picture books and decide which type they are going to write and how they will illustrate the book. With photos? Drawings? Paintings? Students may choose to illustrate their books themselves, or they can ask a classmate for artistic help.

5. When the books are finished, have your students take them to the elementary school and read them to first graders.

Debriefing

Which genre did you enjoy writing the most? Were you sick of your subject by the end of the year? How did your understanding of your subject change over time? What do you know now about research that you didn't know before?

TRY THIS!

BE A HERO AND CHANGE THE WORLD

In the previous research project, the goal is to get passionate, but passion alone will not turn your students into active citizens, so Judy and Joyce teach a passion for service. Their objective is to get the students to realize that they have heroic qualities within themselves, that they have the power to make a difference, even at the age of 11.

Model It

1. Ask the students to define a hero. This is a class discussion. Judy and Joyce read to them from the first chapter of Tom Barron's book *The Hero's Trail*. Barron does a great job of showing that someone doesn't have to be famous to do heroic things.

2. Ask students to name a hero in their own lives. This can run the gamut. Some choose family members, sports heroes, or famous people. Have students write a paragraph about their hero, complete with a picture, which they will display all year in the classroom.

Do It

1. Joyce and Judy discuss their hero, Amy Biehl, who spent the bulk of her short life fighting for the end of apartheid in South Africa. They show students the ABC video *Inside the Struggle: The Amy Biehl Story*. After the film, they ask the students to describe heroic qualities and they list them on a chart. The students are then asked to pick five qualities they feel also describe themselves and tell why in a journal assignment. The process helps children begin to see that they have their own heroic qualities.

2. Display the students' pictures and the words they choose, along with references to their research topics, in the hallway. Keep them up all year long.

3. Show your students the PBS video *New Heroes*, which shows heroes from all over the world, many of them young people, working to alleviate poverty. You can order it from www.pbs.org/opb/thenewheroes.

4. Ask students to find a hero and a cause and take action to be the kind of hero they admire.

Debriefing

What did you learn about yourself from doing this project? Has your view of what is heroic changed? How? What could you do to continue your work on the hero project?

THE NEW BILL

Bill Gates dropped out of Harvard in 1977, the same year I dropped out of college. I went on to finish my degree and become a writer and teacher. He remained a dropout and became the richest man in the world. One gets the feeling Bill Gates does not regret much in his life, but not graduating from Harvard was one of his lifelong regrets. So in the spring of 2007, when he was awarded an honorary doctorate of law at Harvard and asked to present the commencement address, he jumped at the chance. In his eloquent speech, he began by joking about how he was Harvard's most successful dropout, then turned serious and spoke of all he had learned at that illustrious institution about economics, politics, and the sciences. Then, he paused and mentioned "one big regret" he had from his time there: "I left Harvard with no real awareness of the awful inequalities in the world—the appalling disparities of wealth, and health, and opportunity that condemn millions of people to lives of despair."

He went on to tell graduates, ". . .humanity's greatest advances are not in its discoveries—but in how those discoveries are applied to reduce inequity. Whether through democracy, strong public education, quality health care, or broad economic opportunity—reducing inequity is the highest human achievement."

He exhorted the Harvard graduating class of 2007 to do the same thing that Craig Kielburger, Tracy Kendall, and others have done: "take on an issue for life," take a few hours a week and "become a specialist."

Bill Gates may be the richest man in the world, but, in the last few years, he has begun to spend the bulk of his fortune on helping to overcome worldwide poverty. With that, he has gained a different kind of wealth.

I hope this chapter inspires your teaching to grow bigger than the walls of your classroom and helps your students see that writing is more than simply a skill that helps them to succeed in school, but a lifeline to the rest of the planet.

"YEAH, BUT . . ."
Readers' Questions Answered

I have so many curriculum standards to meet and tests to prep kids for. Now you want me to add "saving the world" to the list. I would like to get bigger than the walls of my class, but how do we make time for it?

Okay, stop right there. You are thinking too small. You are thinking either/or. Take a deep breath. Exhale. Now think both/maybe. For example, how do you incorporate persuasive writing into your unit on building a school in Ecuador? Maybe instead of using the state-mandated prompts for writing about whether school uniforms are a good thing or a bad thing, have your students write letters to businesses in town persuading them to donate money for a school project. Ann Barnett, a wonderful middleschool teacher from Houston, Texas, did this. Her students called it the unit that wouldn't end. They raised $4,000 and built a school in Ecuador. You can see the school and the children at freethechildren.com. What did you teach last semester that had this kind of far-reaching impact?

I teach special-needs kids who are lacking in basic literacy skills. How can I justify spending so much class time on projects like this and not following the prescribed lessons I have been given to increase these basic skills?

Recently, research with magnetic resonance imaging scans show that part of a person's pleasure center in the brain lights up when he does something good for another person. Some scientists have concluded that altruism is hardwired into the human psyche. For anyone who has participated in service work, this should come as no surprise. Even though we call special-needs students "developmentally disabled," we still sometimes treat them as handicapped. Opportunities to serve others and engage that altruistic part of our brain can be the single most important thing you do to show your students what life is truly about.

I have so much content to teach in high school English—Shakespeare, Lord of the Flies, To Kill a Mockingbird. *How can I get all that done and do this, too, in just a 45-minute English class?*

Eventually, your school might find that a 45-minute period just doesn't cut it. Refer your administrator to the famous 1994 study "Prisoners of Time," a federally funded study that was conducted to ascertain what is wrong with American high schools. Research showed that time is not the only problem. Schools where teachers need more time tend to do better than schools that transition to block scheduling before they need it. Start teaching as if you have 90 minutes by combining reading and writing instruction. Books like *To Kill a Mockingbird* can be seen as a gold mine of essay-writing ideas waiting to be explored in writing journals.

I teach first grade. How can kids who can barely write participate in these types of social projects? And how can I cover all the skills I'm supposed to teach them?

The key is not to see social projects as extra work. You can incorporate all your skills teaching into these projects. Example: "Today we are going to write a letter to the businesses in town to see if they will donate money to our school. First, I need a report from the treasurer committee. How much money do we have now that we have added the $28 to our $35.42 from the bake sale?" In the movie *Field of Dreams*, the voice said, "If you build it, they will come. . .". In your classroom, "they" refers to your curriculum goals and state standards. If you build it, they will come.

PART III

REFINING WRITING

Like a piece of ice on a
hot stove a poem must
ride on its own melting.

—*Robert Frost*

CHAPTER 9

IT'S DONE . . . NOT!

Learning to Find the "Aha!" Moments of Revision

This is my British friend Miles Bodimeade. I've known him since he was 15, when I was an exchange student in England and boarded with his family. Miles is a gifted artist who went to Liverpool University when he was 17. You can see some of his drawings in this book. Miles also loved literature and kept journals. We used to swap books. Once I gave him George Orwell's *Down and Out in Paris and London*, a memoir of Orwell's journey into the seedy underworld of homeless people in postwar Europe. Miles was so inspired by Orwell's book that he decided to live penniless in London for a weekend and see for himself what it was like to be homeless. He

> Creativity is allowing yourself to make mistakes. Art is knowing which ones to keep.
>
> —*Scott Adams*

came back with tales of all the fascinating people he'd met and a deeper appreciation for the folks you often see begging in the streets.

It is no surprise that today Miles is a screenwriter for the BBC, and is writing his first feature-length film. When I visited him last summer, he showed me the film he had been working on for three months and had revised several times.

We were sitting in his kitchen having a cup of tea and talking when suddenly a blank expression swept over his face. "Aha!"

Miles Bodimeade

Miles exclaimed, and raced to his office to scribble a few phrases on a diagram on his wall.

Miles was revising his movie even as we spoke together. The problem was he had not written a single word of the script yet.

Most teachers of the writing process would say that Miles was still at the prewriting stage, but most writers would know that there is no such thing as prewriting, really. All writing is revision. All revision is writing.

In my first book on writing, *After THE END*, I even went so far as to create a new seven-step writing process.

1. Revision
2. Revision
3. Revision
4. Revision
5. Revision
6. Revision
7. Revision

Here's a cartoon illustration I created to describe this new writing process. The writer in the cartoon grabs an unwritten sentence. His choice revises all his previous choices. All writers are more interested in the stuff that isn't written yet. All writers need tools of the craft to keep them connected with the possibilities that float above their desks. That's where Miles's "Aha!" moment came from and what excites and motivates writers to revise.

My book *Reviser's Toolbox* is a practical guide for students to see new possibilities as they write. Professional writers have a full box of tools that help them to craft new directions, but novice writers do not.

Teachers all over the country tell me that this book helped them to show their students concrete ways to revise their writing, without being formulaic about it.

Grabbing an unwritten sentence

Cathy Walle, a teacher in Michigan, took the tool idea to heart and created a tool apron she uses to introduce each tool.

I will use Cathy's apron in this chapter to show you a few key writing tools and how they have evolved over the years. By the end of this chapter you should have what it takes to start revising with your students.

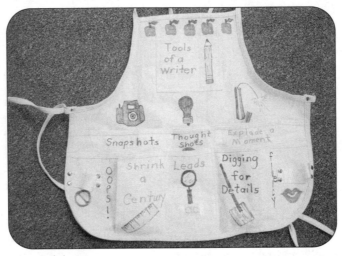

Cathy's apron

DON'T START IN THE BEGINNING—START IN THE MIDDLE

The Roman writer Longinus, who wrote the first how-to book on writing, *On the Sublime*, said it first in Latin: "*in medius res*," or "in the middle." Start your writing at a place of tension. Tell your students that leads are not introductions. Writing is not like life. You don't have to start in the morning to get to the afternoon. You can jump to the good part.

I call the good part "the potato" because the writer and the reader both want to dig it up. Much of what we write is the leaves and the stem of the potato plant, but when you find a really meaningful subject, you start to dig up a potato.

Let's take E. B. White's *Charlotte's Web*. Here is the lead:

> "Where's Papa going with that ax?" said Fern to her mother as they were setting the table for breakfast.

The answer to Fern's question points to Wilbur the pig, who is both the meat and potato of the story.

I ask students why E. B. White didn't start *Charlotte's Web* like this:

"Nice day today, Ma," said Fern to her mother as they were setting the table for breakfast.

They say, "That would be boring." Then, I show them E. B. White's first- and second-draft opening passages for *Charlotte's Web*, which I found in Scott Elledge's biography of E. B. White.

Draft 1

A barn can have a horse in it and a barn can have a cow in it, and a barn can have hens scratching in the chaff and swallows flyin' in and out through the door—but if a barn hasn't got a pig in it, it is hardly worth talking about.

Draft 2

Charlotte was a big gray spider who lived in the doorway of a barn. She was about the size of a gumdrop and she had eight legs and plenty of tricks up her sleeve.

We compare these two leads with "Where's Papa going with that ax?" I ask them, "Why do you think E. B. White chose this lead over the other two?" "It's exciting. It's dramatic. It jumps to the middle of the story and makes you want to read on."

I tell them that not only does a good lead make you want to read on, it makes you want to write on. Let me show you a way to grow great leads from your own curiosity.

TRY THIS!

GROW LEADS FROM QUESTIONS

A lead is a seed from which an entire piece of writing grows. It's not just a first sentence or a flashy hook. In this lesson we learn to grow interesting leads, which start closer to the heart of the story, from our own curiosity.

Model It

1. Start by going to the library or raiding the shelves of the library in your own classroom. Talk to your students about leads. They are not just the first sentence of a piece of writing. They can be a paragraph or two. A good lead

is the perfect start to a piece of writing. Ask a student to take your hand and lead you across the room to demonstrate what a lead does. It leads both the reader and the writer.

2. The other thing about leads is that they raise questions in the reader's mind. Read some "big potato" leads to your students, the kind that get them wondering:

   - I was an untruthful little boy. (*What did he lie about?*)

   - The world for us ended on a Tuesday afternoon in May. (*What happened?*)

3. Next, I tell them a story from my life. I tell them to listen carefully because I want them to ask me curious questions when I'm done. Then, I turn their questions into leads, just as we turned these leads into questions. With young students, I ask them, "Did you ever notice how ears are shaped like question marks? That's because when you really listen, you hear questions." Then I tell a personal story, like this one.

   When I was 11 years old I almost drowned. We were at the lake and my parents had a strange method of swim instruction. They told me, "If you go out over your head, you will drown." No one in my family learned to swim using this method, but I was going to be the first. My parents were sleeping on the chaise lounge chairs and I was staring out at the raft, where younger children were diving and jumping as though laughing in death's face. I made a vow to myself. I'm going out there.

   Now, I knew a few swim strokes from watching Tarzan movies. I couldn't do the crawl, but I could do the Tarzan corkscrew, where you rolled over with each stroke. That one made me dizzy. I could do the backstroke, but one of my arms was stronger than the other and I ended up going in circles. I could make a bit of forward progress doing the hold-your-breath-and-thrash-under-water stroke, only I never came up for air.

   By some miracle, I managed to get out to the raft. I simply willed myself out there. And when I found myself standing on the raft, looking back at the shore where my parents slept on the chaise lounge chairs, my next thought was, "I'm standing on the raft and I don't know how to swim." I then dove back into the water and started swimming madly toward shore, only now I could feel my arms growing heavier and heavier. My legs churned tiny bubbles up all around me. I could see something dark moving toward me, which I soon realized was the bottom of the lake. I could just make out a small newspaper article: BOY, 11, DROWNS WHILE PARENTS SLEEP ON LOUNGE CHAIRS.

"Shouldn't have gone out over his head," they said.

This is it, I thought. I am drowning. As I struggled to get my head above the surface of the water, that's when I saw him.

He sat on a red wooden throne and he wore fluorescent orange swim trunks and had a creamy white nose. He turned his head to one side and slowly walked over to his red surfboard. He paddled out to where I was and when he got a few feet away, he said in a sleepy voice, "So, would you like me to save your life?"

"Sure, glug, glug, glug," I replied.

"Hang on to the board," he said, and then he pulled me forward about five inches, and I could feel the sandy bottom of the lake under my grateful feet.

At this point I turn to the students and ask, "Any questions?"

I list all their questions. We discuss the difference between inside questions and outside questions. Inside questions are about thoughts and feelings. (How did you feel?) Outside questions are about concrete things. (What color was the raft?) Here are some of their questions:

- Why didn't your parents teach you to swim?
- Why didn't your parents swim?
- Why did you jump back in the water when you knew you couldn't swim?
- If you couldn't swim, how did you make it out to the raft?
- What were you thinking when you were drowning?
- Were you scared?

I told my students that I see their questions as gifts to me, because they show me that they have truly listened. They also point me to other places I could begin. If I answer any question in a sentence or two, I have a new lead.

Examples:

Why didn't your parents teach you to swim?

> My parents did not believe in taking any risks in life and they taught me that fear was the best option.

Is this a true story?

> This is a true story.

Do It

Next I say, "Now we are going to try turning questions into leads. When we do this, we jump-start writing to our interest. We find the spark."

- Tell a new story to two partners.

- On a scrap of paper, they will write a question or two for you.

- Have them fold the paper and give the questions back to you.

- Turn one or both of their questions into a lead by simply answering them in a sentence or two. You can't just say yes or no, or begin with a fragment like "because I said so."

- Share your leads with your partners and with the class.

Debriefing

Was it easy to ask questions about one another's writing? What happened when you turned a question into a lead? How can you use this strategy in your own writing? What makes a lead effective? For younger writers: Tell a very sketchy story in one sentence. *Example:*

> It was the happiest day of my life. THE END.

Ask your students if they want to know more. When they say "yes," ask them what they want to know. Write down all their questions on a board.

Examples:

- *What happened?* The day I got my puppy was the happiest day of my life.

- *Why were you happy?* I always wanted a puppy and today I would finally get one.

Tell your students they can start their stories anywhere, but it's good to start close to a place of interest.

TRY THIS!

USING THE BINOCULARS

Have you ever asked a student to expand on something he or she has written, and a week later the student comes back and says, "Here, I wrote bigger. I added more adjectives." The binoculars are a tool you can show your students so that they expand on their own without being asked to. I began to use a pair of binoculars when I found that students of all ages seemed to think that adding details was a blind obligation the writer had to the reader. I wanted students to see that a writer adds details first and foremost to make life more interesting.

Model It

1. Bring a pair of binoculars to class. Ask your students what it's like to look through binoculars when your eyes have not adjusted. They are likely to answer, "fuzzy" or "blurry." Tell them, "That's what it's like when you are describing something at first."

    Example:

    > I walked into the room and there were a bunch of people sitting around. Blurry.

2. Remind your students about the little knob on the binoculars. What happens when you turn it? Things get clearer and more interesting. Here is the secret. You turn the knob as a writer by asking yourself a question about the blurry thing you are trying to describe.

    Example:

    > I walked into the room and there were kids sitting around.
    > *What were they wearing?* T-shirts.
    > *What was on the T-shirts? What color were the T-shirts?*

3. Write a blurry sentence on the board. Here are some examples:

    - He had never seen a messier room.
    - George's meal was disgusting.
    - It was the best day ever.

Do It

1. Ask the students to pick one of your blurry sentences or write one of their own and, with a partner, dig for more specific details by asking questions. "Make a list of all your details and put a star next to your favorite ones."

2. As students share their details with the class, ask them to choose their favorite from the list. See if the class's favorite matches the writer's favorite.

3. Ask your students if they enjoyed digging for details. Talk about how a partner's questions can lead to more interesting details. Tell them, "What your

partners did for you, you can do for yourselves, whenever you get stuck as a writer and everything goes blurry." "What did your partner do for you?"

She asked questions.

Debriefing

Was it fun to use the binoculars? How do details change the more we question them? Can the binoculars help you as a writer? When do you think is the best time to use them? Is there such a thing as writing with too much detail?

THE TWO STAGES OF WRITING WITH DETAIL

kyle thought he was a topic sentence but after ten years of marriage he realized he was just a supporting detail.

As most writing teachers know, it's not enough to teach students to dig for details. We also need to teach them to step back and choose the details that are the most telling. The act of writing is a twofold process.

1. You dig for details.

2. You choose the details that are the most revealing to you.

The first process is easier to teach and learn. The second requires more finesse and understanding. When students choose their favorite detail, they are beginning the process. Another way to teach this is to bring in something old to class or to look at some photos. Below is one of my mom. The other one is the oldest place in North America. No, not St. Augustine, Florida, but Point Hope, Alaska.

My mom

Point Hope, Alaska

Explain to your students that old people, old places, and old things are much more interesting than young people, places, and things. Look at that photo of my mom. Name one or two things about her. Try not to include more than one or two telling details, but those one or two things might say it all about her. Writers call this a thumbnail sketch.

Now look at the house in the other photo. What details jump out at you?

Yes, that is a plane that crashed, and yes, a fellow made it part of his house. That one detail says a lot about Point Hope, Alaska. People use everything up there. If you were describing this town, could you ever ignore that house with the fuselage addition? You may find many more details, but when it comes time to write, you would choose that house.

LANE'S FIRST LAW OF DETAILS

Writing is twofold. First we dig for details; then we choose the details that are the most telling and compelling.

TRY THIS!

THE SMALLEST DETAILS ARE THE FUNNIEST

One of my favorite ways to teach the joy of detail is through comedy. This lesson is for your students who are more interested in getting laughs than getting grades.

Model It

Begin by explaining to your students that the specific detail often gets the laugh. A silly idea becomes funny at the moment it becomes true. Little specific details pin down a big silly idea that is flapping in the wind. One of my favorite ways of modeling this is to show students a matryoshka doll, or nesting doll, like the one pictured on the next page. The big details are the serious ones, but the more you zero in, the smaller and funnier they get. You can model this idea by opening each doll as you model a detail.

- The big detail is that the room is messy.
- Think smaller, more detail. What's the mess?
- There is stuff everywhere.

- Still too broad. What's the stuff?
- There's a pair of dingy tube socks dangling from the overhead fan spinning around and around.

2. After modeling the matryoshka doll, the next step is to take a silly idea and make it funny by adding specific detail.

   Here's a simple way to teach it. Take a school rule or law and flip-flop it by reversing it.

   Example:

   Rule: Never run in the halls.
   New rule: Always run in the halls.

3. Now take the rule and make it funny by coming up with specific (smaller, like the dolls) and true reasons for why we must run in the halls at all times.

4. Share the reasons and look for the laughs.

Copyright ©2003 from 51 Wacky We-search Reports

Debriefing

As the details got closer to the truth, did they get funnier? What are your favorite details? Can you make any one of your details funnier by making it more specific? How can you use what you learned to revise your own writing?

> **LANE'S SECOND LAW OF DETAILS**
>
> Details don't decorate—they animate.

TRY THIS!

IN THE BACKWARDS WORLD

Here is one of my favorite ways of teaching the details that make a concept funny. I have done this lesson with kindergartners and college students, with remarkable results.

In a backwards world, seeds eat birds.

Model It

Tell your students that details animate a silly idea and make it funny. Cartoonists do this in drawing and writers do it with words.

Tell students, "I am going to give you a silly concept, and I want you to take a piece of paper and draw and write details that make this silly idea true."

Here is my silly idea. In the backwards world, everything is backwards.

Do It

Now ask students what they think of the story. When they say, "There is no detail," hand them paper and ask them to create and illustrate one detail for the story.

Debriefing

Did your idea get funnier when you added your details? How does detail improve writing? What makes details work? Where are the best places to use details in a story?

THE TWO PORTRAITS OF LOUIS SEBASTIEN MERCIER

I have a friend in England named Renee. Her great-grandmother was a famous musicologist named Rosa Newmarch, who introduced the work of Tchaikovsky to the British stage. Renee has a box of her great-grandmother's letters from her own grandfather, including her half-written autobiography. It turns out that Rosa Newmarch's grandfather was a famous writer during the French Revolution named Louis Sebastien Mercier. There were two photos of Sebastien Mercier in

Sebastien Mercier

the box. Renee never knew who the man in the two photographs was until she found a brief description of the photos in a letter.

Read the description by Rosa Newmarch and then look at the photos and see if you can identify which photo is which.

I know of two portraits of Sebastien Mercier: one dating from 1789 (when he was 49 years of age and looks younger) appears as the frontispiece to "Sebastien Mercier—Sa vie, son oeuvre, son temps," par Leon Beclard, Paris 1903; the other, taken at a much later date, is still I believe in a French art gallery and a photograph of it is in my possession. There is a marked difference between the portraits. The earlier one shows a good-looking natty man, wearing a neatly-dressed powdered wig of very modest proportions tied in the nape of the neck with a black bow; the forehead is lofty and slightly receding; the lips, well-cut with an upward tilt at the corners, seem to be smiling at some inward joke. The later portrait presented a man of seventy. The eyes are still clear and observant but the wrinkles at the corners have given them more kindness and experience. The elegant lace jabot has given place to a kind of soft Gladstonian collar the points flying in different directions; instead of a neat wig, he has evidently ceased to frequent what he describes in the 'Tableau' as "the abyss of all unseemliness—the Barber's Shop," and wears his own hair framing his handsome head in a soft silvery halo, which adds a benevolent dignity to his striking appearance.

Rosa Newmarch paints a vivid snapshot with words, so vivid that when we see the actual photographs, the match is perfect. The skill of writing with such acute detail has been lost on a culture so heavily dependent on the camera, yet you could also argue that the ability of words to create images is even more valuable today because people are so visually oriented. Here is my favorite lesson for recouping the skill that Rosa Newmarch knew by heart.

But How Do You Teach Writing?

SNAPSHOTS AND THOUGHTSHOTS

A snapshot is a word picture that students can add to or subtract from a piece of writing. A "thoughtshot" is an internal thought, feeling, or reflection that can also be added or subtracted. Knowing the difference between a snapshot and a thoughtshot helps writers to shift gears and improve a piece of writing. I created these two concepts 15 years ago for my first book on revision, *After THE END*, and since then, teachers have told me the terminology has been enormously helpful in teaching skills for accomplishing meaningful and effective revision.

Model It

Talk to your students about two kinds of detail. One type of detail is a snapshot. What is a snapshot? It's a picture from a camera that has more lenses. It can smell and hear things as well as touch things. What is a thoughtshot? It's a thought or a feeling—something internal.

 Example: "If I say 'I was scared,' is that a snapshot or a thoughtshot?" (thoughtshot) "If I say, 'I stand on the edge of the roof,' is that a snapshot or a thoughtshot?" (snapshot) "Simple, right? We are going to practice writing snapshots now."

Do It

1. Ask students to think of a person in their family to write about. (You can also have students bring in a snapshot like the one below and place it on their desks.) Have students follow the steps below.

2. Begin by writing one sentence to locate the person in a specific space and time. "My brother and I sit in a kiddie ride."

3. Look at the sentence and continue writing a small snapshot of that one moment. If you get stuck, turn the knob on your binoculars. Do for yourself what your partners did for you when we did the binoculars lesson.

4. Near the end of your snapshot try adding a thoughtshot of what the person is thinking or what you think about that person or that moment.

5. Share your snapshot with a partner and with the class.

6. Add a snapshot or thoughtshot to a story you are writing.

Me with my brother, Michael

Debriefing

What was it like to write a snapshot? Did you get stuck? Were you able to unstick yourself and write more detail about that moment? How does the writing change when you write a thoughtshot?

```
                        SNAPSHOT

I am lying in my backyard, sun beating hard on my face.  I
hear the birds singing.  I listen to the sounds of my
brothers and cousins playing in the big pool in the back of
our house.  I smile thinking everything in my life is
perfect, then I wake up.  Then I smell the stinky polluted
air.  I look at the people in our small plastic pool.I hear
the birds sing but my cat chases them away.  A fly lands on
my face, I swat at it and hit myself in the nose and I think
this is going to be a long summer.

                        By Chris
```

Chris's snapshot

Chris was a student from inner-city St. Louis who was bused to a suburb for school. In his elegant snapshot he dreams he has a different life and is awakened by reality. Chris's teacher told me that Chris didn't like to write, but the concept of snapshots allowed him to block out distraction and focus on one moment. He eventually learned to add snapshots to his writing.

TRY THIS!

USING SNAPSHOTS, THOUGHTSHOTS, AND DIALOGUE TO BUILD SCENES

Teachers often tell me that their students don't know how to use dialogue effectively in a story. They get stuck in endless tit-for-tat dialogue that goes on for pages and pages. It's hard to tell who is talking and whether the story is going anywhere. Here is a simple way to help.

Model It

1. After teaching snapshots and thoughtshots, ask students what problems they have using dialogue in stories. Usually they will bring up the fact that it gets

boring after a page or so. Tell students you want to show them how to skip the boring bits of dialogue and focus on the good bits.

Here's a simple formula for understanding what a scene is in writing.

Snapshots + Thoughtshots + Dialogue = Scene

This formula simplifies what a scene is, but, for teaching purposes, it's great. I can get rid of ten pages of boring dialogue by simply replacing it with a single snapshot.

Example: They talked for a while and then the bus came.

I can also find a good scene and use a snapshot to rush to it. "They didn't talk much that day, but the next morning at the bus stop Nate said . . ."

Here is a scene I just started writing, with the parts labeled.

> He walked into the room and saw her standing by the soda machine. (snapshot)
>
> "Hi,"(dialogue) he said, trying not to let her know anything was out of the ordinary. (thoughtshot)
>
> "Oh, it's you." She snapped open a can of Diet Coke and some of the fizz hit his cheeks. (snapshot) "I didn't expect you to come to school today." (dialogue)
>
> "I am not really here. It just looks that way." (dialogue) He looked down at the floor, avoiding eye contact. (snapshot)
>
> "Oh, really?" (dialogue) She turned and walked away without saying goodbye. (snapshot)

This scene might end too soon. We want to know what happened. Why is she mad at him? But let's say I wanted to get rid of this scene and replace it with a snapshot. I can do that, too.

> He met her at school in the cafeteria, and she could barely speak to him after spraying Diet Coke accidentally on purpose in his face.

Writers have many choices. Sometimes the choice is whether to write a scene or not. Here are some good reasons to write a scene:

- The scene reveals something about the characters and how they communicate.

- The scene is funny.

- The scene is dramatic.

- The scene shows something important about the story.

Do It

1. Have students separate into groups of three. Tell the class: "Two characters are walking in the woods alone when they find $1,000 in cash. Write a dialogue between the two characters, skipping space to add the snapshots and thoughtshots later."

   Note: Don't let the scene end too soon. Make sure the characters disagree about what to do with the loot.

2. *Optional*: Have each student triad read its scenes with two people playing a character and the third person performing the snapshots and thoughtshots.

Debriefing

What did you learn about your characters in the scene? Can you find a scene in your own writing to cut? Can you find a scene to add to your own writing?

TRY THIS!

EXPLODE THE SLOW-MOTION MOMENT

Filmmakers use slow motion to take the best part of a story and make it last the longest. They pull the reader in with snapshots and thoughtshots and dialogue. Understanding the slow-motion moment in a story can help the writer give shape to piece of writing and add and subtract details. It can also help nonfiction writers pull readers into an essay or report.

Model It

1. Talk to your students about slow-motion moments in movies and in literature. When does an author or a film director decide to use slow motion? Here are some examples.

   • When a character is running to reunite with his sweetheart

   • When a character is diving into a ditch to avoid danger

   • When something is exploding

   • When a character is hitting the game-winning home run

   Why not make the whole movie in slow motion? That would be boring. We pick the special moments to slow down.

2. For fun, try acting out a slow-motion moment with some students from your class.

   • Act it out fast first, and then redo the moment in slow motion.

   • Ask the audience what happened. What do you see in slow motion that you don't see in fast motion?

   • Talk about details and the tools we have already learned for writing in slow motion.

   • Read slow-motion moments from novels and short stories, and even nonfiction books.

Do It

1. Now ask your students, "If you were making a film of your life, where would you use slow motion?" Have them talk with a partner and see how many moments they can think of.

2. Next show your students a piece of paper and tell them you want them to fill the whole page with a moment that lasted only a short time. Don't go to the next day, or the afternoon, but stay inside that one moment. If you get stuck, don't worry. Just say good, I'm stuck, and try using your binoculars. Ask yourself questions. Reread what you have written. If you have written all snapshots, try writing thoughtshots. If you have written all thoughtshots, try adding snapshots.

3. Share the moments.

Debriefing

Did you get stuck or were you able to stay inside the moment? Was it fun to explode a moment? Can you think of moments in your own writing to explode? How did you unstick yourself as a writer? Can you add more to your moment to make it stronger?

TRY THIS!

IT'S SHRINK TIME

Time to a writer is like Play-Doh. You can stretch it out or ball it up whenever you want. In the last lesson we practiced stretching it out; in the next lesson we will practice balling it up.

Model It

Discuss with your students how time is different in writing than in life. When you write, your whole life is like a never-ending sidewalk. You get to skip ahead or go backwards or stand on one square for a day. In real life, you can't skip the boring parts. You live minute by minute, but in writing you can combine ten years into one paragraph or write ten pages about one moment that only lasted a few seconds. Let's practice shrinking a period of time into a paragraph or two. Here are some examples.

From *Charlotte's Web*:

> "The earliest summer days on the farm are the happiest and fairest of the year. Lilacs bloom and make the air sweet, and then fade. Apple blossoms come with the lilacs, and the bees visit around among the apple trees. The days grow warm and soft. School ends, and children have time to play and to fish for trout in the brook."

The beginning of George Orwell's *Shooting an Elephant*:

> In Moulmein, in Lower Burma, I was hated by large numbers of people—the only time in my life that I have been important enough for this to happen to me. I was sub-divisional police officer of the town, and in an aimless, petty kind of way anti-European feeling was very bitter. No one had the guts to raise a riot, but if a European woman went through the bazaars alone somebody would probably spit betel juice over her dress. As a police officer I was an obvious target and was baited whenever it seemed safe to do so. When a nimble Burman tripped me up on the football field and the referee (another Burman) looked the other way, the crowd yelled with hideous laughter. This happened more than once.

1. Begin by finding a block of time to shrink. Write one sentence; for example:

    • The summer at camp was the worst in my life.

    • I discovered video games that winter over Christmas vacation.

2. Now make a list of details from that time on a blank sheet of paper in your notebook.

3. Incorporate your details into a paragraph, shrinking that period of time for the reader.

Debriefing

Was it difficult to shrink time? Did you find an interesting period of time to shrink or were you bored by your writing? What is the advantage of shrinking time to the writer?

Pushing the Fast-Forward Button

One simple way to shrink time is to use what I call the fast-forward button. Here the writer has no interest in shrinking the time so he just skips over it like a movie viewer with a remote control in his hand.

Example:

- Later that day . . .
- Four months later, when he returned from Argentina . . .
- A week later . . .

Spend a few minutes coming up with phrases that propel a story forward, and encourage your students to use these phrases to skip over the boring bits in their writing.

Revising Titles

My father-in-law, Richard Worth, was a brilliant engineer who spent most of his life checking the quality control at nuclear power plants. He spent hours at a time hunched over complicated blueprints looking for possible welding errors, and he was very good at his job. In his youth, he was a merchant marine for two years; then he married and had four children. When he died at age 67, the headline of his obituary read "Merchant Seaman Richard Worth Dies. "

My father-in-law

Because being a merchant seaman was such a small part of Richard Worth's rich life, the headline was absurd. The implication was that it was the most important aspect of his life. Titles and headlines are very powerful because they are the first thing a reader sees. One way to learn the power of titles is to write bad ones.

A BAD TITLE CONTEST

Model It

1. Talk to your students about what makes a good title. Pull books off the shelf of your classroom library and talk about places where authors find titles.

   Examples:

A quote within the text:	*To Kill a Mockingbird*
A central theme or idea:	*The End of Nature*
One word that sums it up:	*Hunger*
A place—Paris 1918:	*The Winter Room*
Name of a character:	*Macbeth*
Summary:	*The Adventures of Huckleberry Finn*

Tolstoy titling his book

copyright 2008 Discover Writing Press www.discoverwriting.com

2. Talk about what a bad title is. A bad title might misrepresent the book or draw attention to the wrong part of the story.

   Example:

   • Instead of *Charlotte's Web*, how about *Templeton Finds Some Cheese*?

   • A bad title might be really vague—instead of *Gone with the Wind*, what about *A Southern Story*?

- A bad title might also be too specific—*Hamlet* might be *The Prince Who Couldn't Make Up His Mind*. (Hey, maybe that's a good title.)

You see, sometimes when trying to write bad titles, we find good titles. Teach your students that brainstorming bad titles can lead to great ones.

3. Ask your class to write some bad titles to books or movies they all know.

4. Share the titles.

Debriefing

What is your worst title? Was it hard writing really bad titles? What makes a title work? What makes a title ineffective? What effect does a title have on the reader?

TRY THIS!

REVISING ENDINGS

Writing endings is tough. Most writers overwrite them and would be better served finding endings in what they have already written.

Don't write endings—look for them! In narrative writing, the ending often grows out of Acts 1 and 2 (the setup and the mix-up). In nonfiction writing, endings are often tacked on like the lid of a jar. How many persuasive essays have you read that ended "In conclusion, here are the main points once again. . ."?

Bottom line: All writers can benefit by developing a sense of daring and flexibility about endings. Teachers can help by teaching and modeling a wide range of endings from literature and life and encouraging students to notice endings, in books, short stories, essays, movies, advertisements, video games, and any other genre. Here is a lesson to help students become conscious of endings in the world.

Model It

Talk to your students about endings. Ask them what makes a good ending in a story, in a movie, in a book. How many types of endings are there? Make a list.

- Happy endings
- Sad endings
- Mysterious endings

- Surprise endings
- Sad but true endings
- Phony endings

Types of endings for essays

- Snapshot endings
- Thoughtshot endings
- End with a scene
- End with a question

Have you ever been to a movie or read a book and been disappointed by the ending? Have you ever loved an ending? Have you ever been disappointed by an ending but felt it was the right ending?

2. Watch a movie with your class and stop it before the ending. Ask them to write two endings to the movie. The first is the ending they think will happen, and the second is a new ending that they create.

3. Share the endings.

Debriefing

Which ending is better, the original or the ending you created? What makes an ending work? What did it feel like to change something that is already written? How does changing an ending change a story?

How to Revise

Here is a reviser's checklist that you can share with your students.

A Reviser's Checklist

- Do I like the lead or can I find or write a better one?
- Where can I use my binoculars to zoom in with more detail?
- Where can I cut detail that does not help my message or story?
- Where can I add or cut a snapshot in my story?
- Where can I explode a moment?
- Where can I shrink time?
- Where can I push the fast-forward button?
- Where can I add or cut a scene?

Give Them the Ball

This is Cody, my 4-year-old cockerpoo, about to play his favorite game, ball. Cody does not play fetch in the normal way. A normal dog chases the ball after you throw it and brings it back. When you throw the ball to Cody, he runs with it, he caresses it in his jaws, and he does a victory dance, like a jubilant football player in the end zone. He may bring the ball back, but only when he is good and ready.

Cody the dog

Snapshots and thoughtshots, leads and scenes are like a chewed-up tennis ball. You will only know their value when your students fall in love with them in their own writing. We want our students to fall in love, to lose themselves in the craft of writing, not play the normal game of fetch-the-assignment. The mini-lessons in this chapter are just the beginning, just the first throw. The end result comes much later when you see your students play with and delight in the craft of their own writing.

"YEAH, BUT . . ."
Readers' Questions Answered

When I teach students to expand their writing they just keep adding more and more words and details, but the writing doesn't improve. Help.

This is very common. Students see detail as simply heaping on adjectives. They need to see that the act of writing with detail is twofold: You dig for details, and then you pick those details that best convey the message you want to convey. One way to teach this is to read thumbnail sketches to students, where an author picks one or two details to convey an impression. Here's one of my favorites, from a fourth grader describing his father.

"My dad is driving our Ford Windstar. He's dancing along to the songs on the radio. My family is yelling at my dad to keep his hands on the steering wheel. He keeps asking, 'Who's the funkiest dad?' No one answers." (From *Reviser's Toolbox*, page 78.)

My students don't want to revise their work because it means they have to do it over.

I am so with your students on this one. I can remember the days before computers when I would type a story over and over again because of a few simple typos. Computers have made us all lazier, and in the best of all possible worlds, students would all have their own computers at their desks. Since we don't live in that world, let's teach students to revise as though they did have a computer. Insert pages into manuscripts, cut and paste paragraphs, make a big, messy, ugly first draft before you get to the do-it-over stage.

Many of the ideas in this chapter seem to be geared to narrative writing. How do I help my students revise nonfiction?

Actually, some of these ideas, like snapshots and thoughtshots, translate very well into nonfiction writing, especially the kinds of nonfiction writing that wants to be read. In an essay, a thoughtshot is an idea or hypothesis (*Global warming is the most important issue of our day*); a snapshot might be a fact (The New York Times *reported that a block of ice the size of Rhode Island broke off from Antarctica last month*). Also, the art of questioning can be a great tool for improving the structure of an essay. Have students write a question for each paragraph in their essay. What question does this paragraph answer? Paragraphs that answer the same question can be cut and other paragraphs might be moved based on the structure of the piece and what the writer is trying to say.

Is it important for primary students to revise their work?

It is important for young writers to see the possibility of revision in their work, even if they revise their story by writing a new one. Concepts like the binoculars, snapshots, and thoughtshots are tools for finding new possibilities. They can practice adding to their work, but I would not make them revise every piece of writing they do. They should walk out of your classroom with simple ways to make their writing stronger.

I believe a student truly learns to revise when they do it on their own. When a student says a piece of writing is done, it is. Our job as teachers is to help them to see on their own that it isn't.

CHAPTER 10

GRAMMAR GOT RUN OVER BY A REINDEER

Teaching Skills in a Fun Context

Here is my first published picture book.

I have gotten letters from students about it and teachers have used it to teach writing. I have been told it is a very funny book that is useful in the classroom. Then I saw this review of my book, from the *School Library Journal*, posted on Amazon.

> Punctuation marks are the road signs placed along the highways of our communication—to control speeds, provide directions, and prevent head-on collisions.
>
> —*Pico Iyer*

The review was fairly neutral until it came to this one sentence:

The run-on plot, in which tortoises and hares try to outsmart one another again and again, is peppered with poor sentence structure and incorrect punctuation.

Ouch! That hurt. I remember the feeling of gut-wrenching disappointment when I

An independent Claus and his friend

read this. It was, sadly, a familiar feeling that I had experienced many times in school when I was handed back a red ink-stained essay. I felt blindsided. I thought I had simply written a story, but instead I had apparently done something terribly wrong. I had offended the grammar gods. This was the same feeling that once made me think I could never be an English major. I imagined there was some secret code they knew that I didn't. And even now, at more than 50 years old, I have written this chapter near the end of the book. Why, because I thought to myself, "What could I possibly teach anybody about grammar and punctuation, when I have a rap sheet three miles long of errors and typos and verbal disagreement?" The margins of my life are filled with red ink.

What bothers me about grammarians is a tendency to flaunt their knowledge of grammar, using it like a cudgel to beat down the ignorant and/or careless masses. It is, I believe, an American version of the class society still so prevalent in Europe and probably why people with British accents are the meanest and best judges on reality shows. America was created to escape the behavior of people like Henry Higgins from *My Fair Lady*, who taught Eliza Doolittle to speak, "The rain in Spain falls mainly in the plain." America is the country where substance trumps form. We thrive on originality and innovation, no matter who you are or where you came from. An American version of *My Fair Lady* might be in reverse. The rapper Kanye West teaches Hank Higgins to get his groove on. Colloquialism is king in the U. S. of A.

Now I hear a chorus of high school English teachers groaning, sighing, heaving this book across the room. How can he say this? Proper communication is essential for a civilized world. The rules of grammar are a prerequisite for proper communication. If teachers don't teach grammar, who will? Eminem? I agree with these statements, and I am not advocating for slipping back into Neanderthal rhetoric. In fact, I believe that English teachers are the sergeants of civilization, the last stop to learn what enlightened discourse might be before the Bill O'Reilly show of life. I am only asking for a little perspective on the subject, and to understand that the rules of grammar are often subject to the needs of what is being expressed. We need to teach students that knowing grammar is akin to knowing a few moves on the basketball court or the dance floor. It gives you flexibility and variety and helps expand your original voice as a writer. You also learn grammar so you don't look like a fool. But writing with conventions does not make you conventional. You are freer to break the rules once you know what they are.

BEST BOOKS ON GRAMMAR

There are many great books on teaching grammar. Probably the best book is still *The Elements of Style* by E. B. White and William Strunk. Strunk was White's teacher in college, and when White became a successful writer, he looked up his old professor and had his publisher print Strunk's self-published handbook on grammar. Another great book on the subject is *Image Grammar* by Harry Noden. Noden teaches grammar through the work of great authors and has his students try on new moves. *Mechanically Inclined* by Jeff Anderson is another amazing resource that attacks grammar from so many angles, and is so easy to use that many teachers will find it an invaluable classroom resource. It also reflects Anderson's wonderful sense of humor.

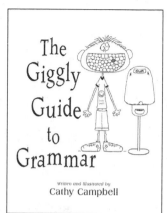

The best teaching books on grammar appear when teachers struggle to find unique ways of reaching their students. One of my favorite ways to do this is through humor, so that's what I am going to teach you in this chapter, along with a basic understanding of how to teach grammar in the context of writing.

In the photo at right is teacher-author Cathy Campbell. I met her at a workshop in Humbolt, Texas, years ago, when two women came up to me and told me there was a woman I had to meet. She was a high school English teacher who drew cartoons of silly sentences to teach grammar to her students, and her students loved her for it. A lot of research shows isolated skill instruction is not effective because students don't remember it. Cathy's outrageous drawings and silly sentences collected in her book for students, *The Giggly Guide to Grammar,* stuck with her students for years because they were so offbeat and funny.

Cathy Campbell

Here is how Cathy teaches transitive and intransitive verbs.

> In this sentence, *juggles* is a transitive verb because it's followed by an object, *mammals*, that receives the action of the verb. *Mammals* answers the question what? after the verb. (Mindy juggles what? Mammals.)

A verb is intransitive if it doesn't have an object. The verb expresses action, but nothing in the sentence receives the action.

Mindy juggles for her friends.

In this sentence, juggles is intransitive because you can't answer the question whom? or what? directly after it. Therefore, it has no object that receives its action. Instead, the verb is followed by a prepositional phrase.

Reprinted from The Giggly Guide to Grammar
Discover Writing Press copyright 2008

TRY THIS!

"GIGGLERIZING" GRAMMAR INSTRUCTION: THE SILLY SENTENCE METHOD

Making silly sentences is a great way for you and your students to playfully learn the rules of grammar. Silly sentences that your students write help them to remember the concept.

Model It

Tell your students you want them to remember certain rules of grammar by making up the craziest sentences you can think of to exemplify the rule.

Example:

Domenica raises earthworms, and she teaches them amazing tricks. Concept: Use a comma and a conjunction to join two independent clauses.

1. Pass out oversized index cards to your students. Pick a grammatical concept and create a silly sentence. Write the rule of grammar on the lined portion of the card

Reprinted from The Giggly Guide to Grammar
Discover Writing Press copyright 2008

and then flip it over. Write your sentence and illustrate it on the blank side of the card.

2. Have your students do a silly sentence card each time they learn a new grammatical concept.

3. By the end of the year, students will have their own deck of cards. Scan and send your silly sentences to barry@discoverwriting.com, and I will post them on my Web site.

4. Collect all your students' cards and create a deck. Then shuffle them so the silly sentence side faces up. Divide the class into teams and take turns reading the silly sentences and trying to identify the rule in question.

5. Keep score of which team identifies the most rules.

Debriefing

Do you like your grammar rule? Do you think you will remember it? How does writing a silly sentence help us to remember?

TRY THIS!

FUMBLE RULES FOR GRAMMAR

I first learned this from a column by William Safire. The idea is to create a grammar rule book, but you break every rule when you describe it in a sentence. Fumble-rule books create the kind of cognitive dissonance that makes you remember something (and work especially well, if kids have their own books).

Model It

1. Begin by creating some fumble rules and putting them on the board or overhead projector. Here are some examples:

   the first word of every sentence must begin with a capital letter.

   Join two independent clauses with either a conjunction and a comma or with a semicolon.

   Ask students what they notice in the grammar rules. Someone will say that the mistake is made in the rule.

2. Tell your students you want them to create their own fumble rules for grammar. Have them state a rule of grammar, while breaking the very rule discussed, in a sentence. Here are some grammar rules to help your students get started.

   - Join two independent clauses with either a comma followed by a conjunction or a semicolon.

   - Use commas to bracket nonrestrictive clauses that are not essential to sentence meaning.

   - Don't use commas to bracket phrases essential to the meaning of a sentence.

   - Include a comma after an introductory clause at the beginning of a sentence.

   - Make the subject and the verb agree with each other, not with the word between them.

   - Use parallel construction to make a strong point and make the writing flow.

   - Write in active voice unless you have a reason not to.

   - Omit unnecessary words.

3. Create fumble-rule posters around the class. Try combining silly sentences from the last lesson with this one and see what happens.

Debriefing

Which of your fumble rules do you like the best? What grammatical error are you most prone to making in your writing? How do fumble rules help us remember the rules of grammar?

TRY THIS!

HANDING OVER THE PENS OF POWER

When I was in school, teachers wrote strange marks in red ink all over my work. They were called editing symbols, but we didn't know that back then. I thought they just had a strange code that they were unwilling to share with us. Research shows that it does not help to correct every error the student makes. It's better to hand over the editing pen to the people who need the most practice editing—your students. But how do we begin the process at any grade level?

Model It

1. Talk to your students about editing and correcting. Tell them that you need their help editing a piece of writing. Put your piece on the overhead and ask them to find the errors. When they call out an error, talk to them about the the editing symbol designed to mark or correct that error. Each time you teach a new symbol, put it up on a chart.

2. When you have taught editing symbols like this for a few lessons, you are ready to hand over the editing pen to your students.

3. Create some type of ritual to make this fun. Maybe buy red pens for the whole class and create some kind of editing ceremony where you give them the "pens of power." Editing hats are also a great way to create a separation between editing and writing. They can practice editing sentences in their notebooks or in their writing.

Debriefing

What is it like to have the pen of power? How does editing help you to see your writing in a different way? Is there a difference between an error and a mistake? What are your most common errors?

The Psychic Sasquatch Meets the Poor Proofreader

When I was in my early 30s, I took a job at a new age publisher as an editorial assistant reviewing manuscripts like "The Psychic Sasquatch." Since I had a master's degree in English and was about to publish my first book on teaching writing, my employer assumed I was a competent proofreader. Nothing could have been further from the truth. I have never lied at a job interview before, and luckily they didn't ask me. In time, my dismal proofreading skills would emerge. Luckily, Anna, the woman who shared my office and worked on the weekends editing medical textbooks for fun, agreed to have a second look at some of the proofreading tasks handed over to me. With her help, I stayed at that job at least two months longer than I should have. Occasionally, I would watch Anna

THE LANGUAGE OF EDITING

The standard copyediting symbols will help you to change your work so that editors will know what your correction marks mean. Learn them and use them.

Symbol	What it means	Example
∧	Insert/add something	I ∧need you. *(really)*
ℓ	Delete something	I really need you.
#	Add space here	Ireally need you ∧
↗	No space here/close gap	I really need you
⌐¶	New paragraph	"Why," I asked. "Because.. ¶
⌐	No paragraph	I really need to know.⌐ Will you tell me?
～	Reverse order	Will you tell me. I really need to know.
≡	Make this a capital letter	Dear bob, ≡
/	Make this a small letter	What /Are you doing?
⊙	Insert a period	They went to the park∧She ⊙
⟪ ⟫ ∧ ∧	Insert quotation marks	⟪Hello, she said⟫ ∧ ∧
⌄	Insert apostrophe	Sharon⌄s coat was on . . .

proofread after I handed her a press release. She held a pencil in her right hand and raked it over each line on the paper. When she got to the end she started all over again, and then a third time. Once I asked her why she read a piece so many times and she replied, "The first time I read it for capitalization and punctuation, the second time I read it for spelling, the third time I read it for anything I missed the first two times." It was clear that Anna knew the secret of a good proofreader: focus. In this next section, we learn how to hand over the editing pen to your students and use focus as a tool.

Following is a proofreading checklist for your students. Have your students practice looking for particular errors.

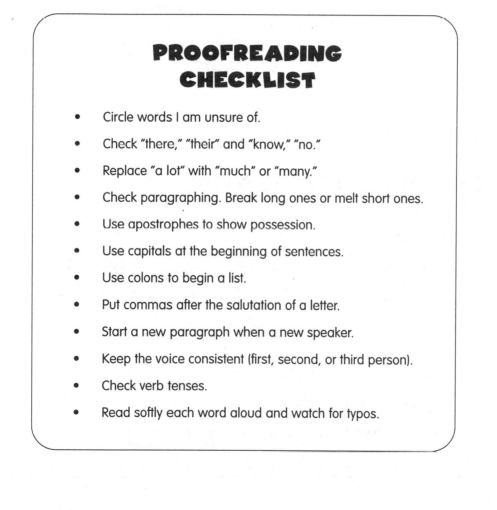

PROOFREADING CHECKLIST

- Circle words I am unsure of.

- Check "there," "their" and "know," "no."

- Replace "a lot" with "much" or "many."

- Check paragraphing. Break long ones or melt short ones.

- Use apostrophes to show possession.

- Use capitals at the beginning of sentences.

- Use colons to begin a list.

- Put commas after the salutation of a letter.

- Start a new paragraph when a new speaker.

- Keep the voice consistent (first, second, or third person).

- Check verb tenses.

- Read softly each word aloud and watch for typos.

Model It

1. When student have studied punctuation for a while, tell them they are ready to have some fun with it. They are going to invent their own punctuation marks.

2. Encourage them to choose a name that tells what a particular mark does. A period might be a "sentence-stopper." A comma might be a "phrase joiner." Have fun and be creative.

3. Have students punctuate a piece of writing with their new marks, and share it with another student.

4. Students swap papers and assume the rule of archeologists whose job is to figure out the meaning of the new punctuation marks from context clues and then create a translation chart showing the meaning of each mark.

Debriefing

What did you learn about punctuation by creating your new marks? What is the purpose of punctuation?

MY FAVORITE ERRORS

Writers need to be aware of the kinds of errors they make to become better editors and proofreaders. When students keep track of their favorite errors, it helps them become aware of their common mistakes so they can easily spot them in their writing. Have them include this chart in their writing folders.

> ### My Favorite Errors List
>
> i forget to start with a capital letter
>
> I put, commas in the wrong, places.
>
> I join two independent clauses with a comma, I do it all the time.

PRINCE PERFECT LEARNS TO WRITE

This is a great way to teach your students the importance of simple prose. I originally published a version of this idea in my first book, *Discovering the Writer Within*, cowritten with Bruce Ballenger. Back then I called it the "William F. Buckley Shoe Shuffle," after the famous conservative talk-show pundit who was known for his massive vocabulary. Over the years, I have experimented with this lesson in the younger grades and replaced Buckley with "Prince Perfect," a refined individual with a large vocabulary.

Model It

1. Talk to your students about the differences between formal writing and informal writing. In formal writing you use bigger words, but formal writing need not be overblown and bombastic. You just don't use colloquial speech. It's a bit like wearing a fancy dress or a tuxedo. Informal writing is jeans and a T-shirt. Practice with some phrases.

   Informal: The dog dropped the slipper in the potty.

   Formal: The canine deposited the casual footwear in the toilet.

   Exaggerated formal speech uses many more words. One way to practice this is to take a simple sentence like this one and inflate it:

   The cat spent the night in the car.

   Try a quick contest. See how many words your students can put into one sentence, without changing the meaning or repeating words like "very, very, very."

2. Now we are going to imagine a character. Close your eyes. Imagine, if you will, Prince Perfect and Princess Perfect. They are dressed in their finest evening wear, walking hand in hand down the lane, when both of them simultaneously step in dog doo.

3. Afterward, in a letter to a friend describing the event, they are so prim and proper they can't use any crude words. Encourage your students to come up with creative ways of describing the unpleasant concepts.

4. Share your Prince and Princess Perfect letters. Delight in how your students

creatively use language to dress up the experience with terms like "organic canine rubble."

5. Imagine you are a cab driver or a farmer, someone who likely speaks in plain language. You have just witnessed the prince and princess's misstep and are telling a friend about it. Using informal language, describe how you would tell a friend about this incident.

Debriefing

In which voice did you feel more comfortable writing? How did your writing change when you wrote in each voice? Is the formal voice better? Is the informal voice better? What did you learn about language from this lesson?

THE EDITOR AT THE IN-SERVICE DAY

Once while I was presenting a professional development workshop on the topic of this chapter, a high school English teacher came up to me at break time and told me that she corrected every single grammatical error in her students' papers and wouldn't have it any other way. Was I telling her she was wasting her time? I paused for a moment and thought how I should answer. Then I decided not to answer the question at all. Instead I asked her, "Well, what do you think?"

She looked me straight in the eye and said, "They just don't care."

"Okay," I said, "then maybe that is where we need to start."

I hope this chapter has given you some ideas for engaging students in the study of language and grammar and developing appreciation for the role it plays in writing. I hope that with the help of these pages, you can create and teach grammar lessons that will last a lifetime.

"YEAH, BUT . . ."
Readers' Questions Answered

I put a sentence on the board with errors each day and ask kids to correct the errors and speak about them. Does this help students learn grammar?

Research says activities like this don't have a lasting effect on the student's own writing, but it may help them to succeed on tests that ask the same kinds of questions. I think it's a fun way to get your students to focus on grammar, especially if your sentences focus on something going on in the school that day. Try some "giggly" sentences, too (see pages 169–171).

Does it help to correct students' grammatical errors? I feel guilty when I don't.

Don't feel guilty. Correcting grammar is not always your job; teaching students how to do it is your job. Rather than correct each error, look for a pattern of error, correct a few, and ask your students to find the rest. Hand over the mighty pen of power.

How do you teach vocabulary? Should you?

Traditional vocabulary tests and memorization of lists just doesn't work. In her book *Vocabulary Unplugged,* Alana Morris teaches a love of words and brain strategies like word walls and wordstorms that give students confidence in the words they already know. My favorite technique is vocabulary charades. Instead of giving a verbal definition for the word, give a muscle definition, a gesture, or a facial expression. Practice it with the class and have them memorize it. Then write the definition on the wall and have kids match it to the list of words.

I teach first grade, and my students barely know letters. How can I get them excited about punctuation?

I learned a fun method from Patricia Pierce and her forthcoming book, *The Punctuation Quarrel.* It's called personifying punctuation. In Pierce's book, punctuation marks argue over who is the best. Their personalities betray their function.

> *Example:* Wait!" shouted Eddy Exclamation Point. "Why are you always shouting?" asked Clara Question Mark.

Teach your students the function of punctuation marks by having them create characters who personify each mark. Have fun making punctuation plays.

CHAPTER 11

YOU DON'T FATTEN A PIG BY WEIGHIN' IT, DO YOU?

Making Assessment and Testing Work for Your Students and for You

ifty Education Way is a newly paved road that runs through a field off Fifth Street in Dover, New Hampshire, the town where I grew up. When I was 12 years old I drove my gold Schwinn Stingray past that field on the way to a local pond for my first overnight fishing trip with my best friends Mark, John, and Rick. We didn't get a single nibble that day and I lost two fishing lures in the weeds, but looking back, I realize it was still a successful trip.

> Every compulsion is put upon writers to become safe, polite, obedient, and sterile.
>
> —*Sinclair Lewis*

It was all the anticipation, the sleepover, the getting up at dawn, and all the playful, boyish camaraderie that made that trip so memorable. My friends and I talked about it for years. A few bony and barely edible pickerel would not have sweetened the deal much.

As I drive down Education Way, the road cuts through the open fields of my childhood and bends

50 Education Way

around a corner, to reveal huge brick buildings. They look a bit like schools, except for the well-groomed corporate lawns and absence of playing fields and fences. It is summer and there is a conspicuous absence of cars and people. In a few short months, a thousand temporary workers will come here each day to score writing tests from 20 states.

It's odd that there is no sign out front. It is only when I walk through the glass doors that I see the enormous sign that reads "Measured Progress" and the motto "It's all about student learning. Period."

My first thought is, Are we getting a little defensive here? Isn't the jury still out on testing? Is testing really all about learning? Or is it also about control? Money? Power? Politics?

Pat, the public relations person for Measured Progress, is a friendly mother of two and a professional writer. I immediately like her. She gives me my badge, and we move through security. She tells me that once when she forgot her badge, a temp worker at the desk didn't recognize her and she was not allowed in the building. They take security very seriously at Measured Progress.

On the way to her office, we pass the empty summer cubicles. Pat and I talk a bit about testing. She says she doesn't understand when she hears parents complain that teachers are teaching to the test. She points to her own two children in New Hampshire schools and how their essay writing has improved as teachers spend more time preparing for the state test. "Some call it teaching to the test," she says. "I call it teaching writing."

I tell her that I am not sure that all test prep helps students develop as writers. Tests are like big motorboats that leave waves of quick-fix instruction in their wake, promising higher scores to panicked administrators and sending ripples through school systems. Only the most knowledgeable administrators can stand up and say, "Enough is enough." I have seen first graders being drilled in the ubiquitous hamburger paragraph before they even knew what a sentence was. But I am not anti-test. I have seen a huge rise in the teaching of writing since the testing craze hit the schools, so it can't be all bad. My work on Vermont's portfolio assessment program showed me that the right kinds of assessments can drive instruction in a positive direction and encourage the teaching of writing craft.

When I meet with Vince and Karin, two senior scorers at Measured Progress, I am reminded of those early years in Vermont. They are both sincere, dedicated people who truly believe that testing helps children become better writers. I tell them that I often have children draw pictures of test scorers, and I don't see any resemblance.

Their goals are to set standards and improve schools so that students can be successful in life. Measured Progress is careful to hire well-qualified scorers,

Vince of Measured Progress   Vince's colleague Karin

many of whom have had teaching experience, and their training is rigorous
and controlled.

Most papers are double-scored, and a team leader moderates any discrepancy,
casting a deciding vote. They refer to "anchor papers" picked by teachers
whenever there is doubt about a score. But there is one strict rule at Measured
Progress that occasionally gets broken even by the most seasoned and devoted test
scorers. Scorers are not allowed to talk about the writing when they take a break,
but both Karin and Vince guiltily admit there is an uncontrollable urge to want
to share the contents of a wonderful essay with a fellow scorer.

When I ask Vince if he can think of such a memorable paper, a grin spreads
over his face. He describes a ninth grader who answered the prompt "Write about
a special person in your life" by describing a zombie. The piece was filled with
brilliant descriptive detail, right down to the flesh on his face flapping in the wind.
As Vince describes the paper, I realize something. His voice has changed. When he
talks about the testing process his voice was low, controlled, almost a whisper, but
when he talks about the zombie paper, his voice brims with enthusiasm, and his
face beams like a teacher describing the work of a favorite student.

Karin says that some of the most interesting writing they see are refusals—
students who write about how the test is dumb. But even though it is clear these
are wonderful writers, in most states these papers cannot be scored because they
are considered off-topic. In other words, if you reject a test topic, you are
considered a failed writer. A student who thinks a test prompt is dumb, but
complies with it, is considered a successful writer. Are we testing writing or are
we testing compliance?

Pat tells me her college-age daughter had tried her hand at being a test scorer
and failed miserably because she kept trying to score the potential in a piece of
writing and not what was on the page. She was too empathetic, too much of an
encouraging teacher to be an objective evaluator.

That's when it hits me. No matter how much we would like it to be otherwise, tests promote uniformity, whereas writing teachers, at their best, promote endless diversity. At some level, testing and teaching are diametrically opposed activities.

LANE'S TRUTHS OF TESTING

- Tests promote uniformity. (Non-compliant writing is often not scorable.)

- Tests promote failure. (If everyone passes the test, it is too easy.)

- Teachers promote diversity. (They want to reach all students.)

- Teachers promote success. (Teachers want all their students to succeed.)

In 1987, in his classic *Joining the Literacy Club*, Frank Smith wrote:

> The ultimate response to people opposed to the massive evaluation that invests education today is, 'Don't you want children to learn?' No one should get away with a loaded question like that. Proponents of testing and grading should be challenged to demonstrate exactly how they expect evaluation to improve learning and teaching and to avoid all the undesirable consequences. There is no evidence that external control leads to better teachers or to better learners. There is a wealth of evidence to the contrary.

In the years since Smith wrote this, the standards movement has taken up his challenge and tried to prove that testing improves learning. Unfortunately, the only way to prove anything is to do more testing. So we test students to find out if tests are working? Does anyone see a problem with this model? My seventh-grade daughter, Gracie, did. She was required to write the number of each state educational standard her teacher was meeting with each assignment she was completing for homework.

"Dad, I don't believe it," she once said to me in the car on the way home from school. "It's like we have to help the teacher prove to her boss that she is teaching." I couldn't really disagree. Gracie picked up on the climate of paranoia and micromanagement that has become prevalent in education since the standards movement. I have been to schools recently where, instead of student writing on the walls, you see data and flow charts. I have heard principals describe themselves as "data-driven." Whatever happened to real learning?

No matter how much the powers that be would like it to be, testing is not the path to improving a school: teaching is. Or to put it in the lingo of Measured Progress: *It's all about teaching. Period.*

Or as the Kentucky pig farmer put it: *"You don't fatten a pig by weighin' it, do you?"*

So how do we get our students engaged with thinking and writing, and avoid what author George Hillocks calls "the testing trap"? How do we make education a journey to knowledge and not a fishing trip valued only for the number of fish caught?

In this chapter I'm going to show you a few creative dance moves that help sidestep the test and at the same time get great results. I will also show you how to create your own meaningful, practical writing assessment with your students.

TRY THIS!

DRAW THE TEST SCORER BEFORE AND AFTER

Here is a lesson from my DVD *Hooked on Meaning*. It is a wonderful lesson to try with students the week before the test because it helps to level the playing field. After you do the assignment you can scan the images students draw and create a slide show. You can see clips from *Hooked on Meaning* and a three-minute slide show of students' drawings of test scorers at my YouTube channel: barrylane55.

DUANE REVERTED TO PROMPTED TEST TALK WHENEVER HE GREW NERVOUS ON A DATE.

copyright 2008 Discover Writing Press www.discoverwriting.com

Model It

1. Talk to your students about what it must be like to score writing essays all day long. As people read these essays, what goes through their heads? What do they think? If it were your job, how would you feel about it? Often, students remark how boring it must be reading essay after essay.

2. Role-play. Have a student come before the class and put on a pair of nerd glasses. Have the student pretend to be the test scorer and comment on the student essays. Here are some of the comments students make:

But How Do You Teach Writing?

- Why are they all the same?

- Am I reading the same one over and over?

- I need a new job. . . .

Talk to your students about how boring this job could be. Tell them that the scorers could lose their jobs, and their duty is to keep the test scorer awake!

3. Draw a picture of the test scorer who will read your test. Next, draw a picture of the same test scorer after he or she has read your test. How did the scorer change?

Drawing of test scorer by Robert, a ninth grader

Debriefing

How did the test scorer change? What can you do as a writer to wake up the test scorer? Will waking up the test scorer get you a higher score?

Lessons in test success from the Great Gretchen

Let me introduce you to Gretchen Bernabei. She is a brilliant teacher whom I met in Texas years ago. I attended a short workshop she was giving and was immediately taken by how much I wanted to be in her class. It's a sad, grief-stricken feeling I get every so often when I find myself in the presence of great teachers. If only she would put me on the waiting list, I could try to get in today. I would be her best student. (I could try to blend in.)

What makes Gretchen so special is that all her lessons grow out of what she has observed about how her students learn, mixed with a deep understanding of language theorists like Lev Vygotsky and Mikhail Bakhtin. Her book *Reviving the Essay: How to Teach Structure Without Formula* is the only book I have seen that shows teachers how to teach students to succeed on writing tests while at the same time promoting good writing. Gretchen's lessons work as test preparation but they are just as valuable for helping students become good writers. Let me show you what I mean.

Me with Gretchen Bernabei

STEP AWAY FROM THE PROMPT AND FIND YOUR TRUTH

(Adapted from Reviving the Essay *by Gretchen Bernabei)*

Psychometricians will tell you that a good writing prompt is one that generates a wide range of responses. Yet even good writing prompts will draw poor responses if students don't know how to make the prompt their own. Here's a lesson straight out of Gretchen's playbook on how to inspire students to personally interpret the prompt and find their truth. Gretchen has created a CD-ROM of images called "Lightning in a Bottle" to introduce her students to the concept of truisms, or obvious, self-evident truth. You can use Gretchen's images or create your own overheads to teach this lesson.

Model It

1. Put a truism with a photograph on the overhead or LCD or, in a small class, just show it to the students. Show them the sentence and ask them if they think it's true. Then show the photo. How does it relate? Do this a few times to get the feel of it.

2. Show them the photograph without the truism. Ask them, "What's going on in the photo?" Then ask, "What's one true thing about the world that this photo shows?" Celebrate the truths they come up with. Hang their ideas around the room. Talk about how diverse and wonderful each one is.

3. Say, "This time I am not going to show you a truism or a picture, just plain words; life has all kinds of adventures."

   Have students draw a picture of what the words make them think. Then have them write a few truths about their drawings.

4. Ask students to pick one of their truisms and free-write about it. Ask them to write about how it relates to books they have read, movies they have seen, and other events in their life.

Debriefing

If a truism is true to me, is it true to everybody? What is truth? How does finding my own truth in a writing prompt help me? Where will this truth take my writing?

You never know how high you'll go until you jump!

Truisms From Fourth Grade

The future is locked until its moment. —Wesley

Everyone has a secret. —Brandon

Even something so small can make a big difference. —Sallie

Small things can hold everything together. —Lindsey

If you do drugs, you'll get locked-up. —Donald

There's always a key in life. —Jessica

Everyone gets in trouble. —Brandy

from Reviving the Essay *by Gretchen Bernabei. Used with permission.*

TRY THIS!

PICK A STRUCTURE, ANY STRUCTURE

(Adapted from Reviving the Essay *by Gretchen Bernabei)*

Once you have a truth and something to say, the next step is to find a structure for your essay. Traditional textbooks teach one basic structure, the five-paragraph theme, a form that exists only in schools, when there are many structures to choose from, it's like handing students a box of crayons and asking them to pick a color to go with their ideas. Teaching structure this way helps students see that structure grows out of self-expression and not the other way around. This lesson, the story of my thinking, is one of my favorites because it teaches what Thomas Newkirk means when he says that essays track the movement of the mind. It shows students that, like good stories, essays often end at a different place than where they start.

Model It

1. Model this basic structure for your students: I used to think _____.
   Then this happened: _____. Now I think _____.
   Here's mine:

   > I used to think that I had a poor sense of direction, but too many times I have two maps and a GPS and I still end up going the wrong way. Now I wonder if, at some level, I enjoy the uncertainty of being lost.

   This is what Gretchen calls a kernel essay—a seed from which an entire essay can grow.

2. Tell your students, "I'm going to show you how to find a kernel essay, or seed essay, and plant it on a piece of paper." Give each student three index cards and have them number them 1, 2, and 3. Then write a statement of truth on an overhead or chalkboard. It might be a general truth or a more personal truth, but it should be one that experience has taught you is true.

This is your Brain.

This is your brain writing a school essay.

copyright 2008 Discover Writing Press
www.discoverwriting.com

Do It

1. Look at the statement on the board. Think of some truth of your own, an understanding that has evolved or changed over time. Write your truth on card number 3.

2. Now think about your truth. What happened to make your ideas change? On card number 2 write down one event from your life that showed you this statement was true. Write for three minutes, putting as much detail in as you can.

3. You have only one card left now—number 1. Use it to write what you used to think about the truth on card number 3 before the events on card number 2 happened.

4. Look at your three cards and write a few sentences in the structure I modeled for you earlier. I used to think _____. Then this happened: _____. Now I think _____.

Example:

> I used to believe in Santa, but I was up all night peeking out the other door, and I got in trouble. Now I think we will pretend that he is real because of the little kids. —fourth grader

(See examples of more text structures at www.trailofbreadcrumbs.com)

Debriefing

What is the relationship between the number 1 card and the number 3 card? Was it difficult to word the number 1 card to show the changes? When you look at your kernel essay, what ideas do you have about how you could turn it into a real essay?

TRY THIS!

BA-DA-BING: GIVING RELUCTANT WRITERS SOME TRACTION

Reluctant writers have a hard time getting going. Their writing is often composed of short, disconnected sentences. Like a car stuck in sand, spinning its tires deeper into a rut, they don't go anywhere. Gretchen Bernabei invented this really cool way to help push reluctant writers onto the highway of meaning. Here's how to teach Ba-Da-Bing.

Model It

1. Give your students a piece of paper and ask them to draw a foot, an eye, and a thought bubble (like in a cartoon).

2. Show your students a writing prompt and/or a photo with a truism. Ask them to think of a time that the photo or prompt reminds them of. Have students write a sentence that begins with where their feet took them, and then says what they saw and what they thought.

Examples:

Teacher Prompt:

> I went to back to the old house on Highland Street where I grew up, saw my bedroom high above the driveway, and thought to myself how isolated I lived from the rest of the world.

Student Responses to a Prompt:

> I walked into the kitchen and saw my mother holding a skateboard and I thought, Hey is that for me! —Torrey, 2nd grade

> When I was sitting quietly in the room I saw him walk in and thought, "Oh please! Don't let it be me! Please, oh please!" —Rhia, 4th grade

> When I stepped onto the stage, I couldn't see the audience because the lights were in my eyes. What was I so afraid of? I thought. "This is fun!"
> —Matilde, 6th grade

3. Each of your students' Ba-Da-Bing sentences can be a small kernel essay. Ask them to try expanding it by connecting it to things they've read, movies they've seen or other experiences in their lives and writing about it.

Debriefing

Do you like your Ba-Da-Bing sentence? Were you able to expand it? Where did you find support for your ideas? How does your writing relate to the prompt? Where did it take you?

TRY THIS!

THE CRITIC ON YOUR SHOULDER

(From Why We Must Run with Scissors: Voice Lessons in Persuasive Writing 3–12 *by Barry Lane and Gretchen Bernabei)*

Once your students have the basic structure of an essay, they can start to work on developing it. Traditional books prescribe listing three supporting details, which often turns students' writing into a list of details or, worse, the same detail repeated three times. When Gretchen Bernabei taught 12th graders in Texas, the state had a persuasive writing test that you had to pass to get out of high school. When students failed, they were sent to Gretchen, who taught them this one lesson. Gretchen calls it the "Jerk on Your Shoulder." When I work with younger students, I call it the "Doubting Chorus."

Model It

1. Tell your students that an essay is a conversation between a writer and an invisible audience. In persuasive writing, the audience is a doubting audience that the writer is trying to convince, but this might also be true of all writing that is convincing and real.

2. Tell your students they are going to teach their audience to be doubters.

You:	Global warming is real.
Critic:	No, it's not.
You:	Yes, it is
Critic:	No, it's not.
You:	Yes, it is.
Critic:	Prove it
You:	CO_2 levels correspond with rising temperatures through history. In the last 20 years, CO_2 levels have skyrocketed. A piece of polar ice twice the size of Texas did not freeze last year.
Doubters:	You're wrong. How do you know that?
You:	It was reported in the documentary *An Inconvenient Truth*. And most all scientists believe that study, even those who didn't vote for Al Gore.

3. Tell your students that the only way to quiet the critic on their shoulder is with facts, with documented sources. When you reread your writing, let the critic on your shoulder doubt your words, then elaborate with facts and details to quiet him. The art of elaboration comes naturally when you respond to the doubting voice.

Debriefing

Was it fun to be the critic? Were you able to elaborate in your writing by quieting the critic? What is the difference between a fact and an opinion? How can this help you when you are writing an essay on a test?

THE THREE A'S OF TESTING

Lately I have been asked to present workshops on how to help students quickly succeed on writing tests. After a lot of thought I came up with the three As of testing.

Audience: a sense of who you are writing to and the ability to connect with your readers

Animation: a liveliness in the writing that comes from personal connection to the prompt

Artfulness: an understanding of the craft of writing

So far in this chapter we have touched on the first two A's. The third A, artfulness, was addressed in Chapter 7. Another way to understand craft is to teach your students to assess their own writing.

TRY THIS!

SNOW WHITE AND THE SEVEN TRAITS: EXPLAINING ASSESSMENT TO STUDENTS

Some teachers are required to do an assessment program such as six traits, as well as state assessments, while others might have school assessments. I feel that whatever assessment we do, we must begin by teaching the concept of assessment to our students. Assessment comes from the Latin verb *assidere*, to sit beside. Assessment is not ranking. It is describing.

Model It

1. Tell your students you want to create and design a writing assessment guide with them. You want to come up with a way to quickly describe a piece of writing. Talk to your students about what makes good writing, and that before you assess writing, you are going to assess bubblegum. Elicit from your students some criteria for bubblegum, and list them on the board:

   - Sweet flavor
   - Big bubbles

- Bubbles don't stick to your face when you pop them
- Long-lasting

Create a simple assessment guide by placing the criteria in the left-hand column and writing four numbers across the top: 1 2 3 4

2. Ask students to copy the guide onto a piece of paper. Next hand out three types of bubblegum and, in groups of two or three, have them assess the bubblegum for each criterion by drawing a line across the page to see which criterion is in the lead.

3. Compare the results and discuss reasons why people didn't agree on which was best. Tell them that we don't always agree on everything, but assessment is an attempt to objectively describe something. It will never be exact, and it is only useful if it helps you to see ways of improving your writing.

4. Next, ask this question, What is good writing? Here is a typical class brainstorm. Good writing is:
- Details that make you feel like you are there
- Humor
- You can't put the book down.
- The author makes you keep reading.
- Endings that stick with you
- Interesting characters
- Plots that keep you guessing

5. At this point you can take a standard rubric like the six traits and connect it with your students' observations. Some likely connections:
- Interesting characters correspond with idea development
- Humor corresponds with voice.

Show your students that the assessment guide is a way of reducing writing to simple qualities.

6. Next, assess a piece of writing using Barry's Favorite Rubric (below) or the same guide you used to assess the bubblegum. Fill in the name of each trait you come up with at the bottom of the page and assess the writing. Make sure you include qualities of writing such as humor that are not on the standard rubric. This will help nail home the point that assessment is not

ranking; it's describing. For example, "Let's assess the memos from the superintendent's office for humor. Hmm . . . you might find a low score there."

Barry's Favorite Rubric

I designed this rubric while standing in front of the Bellagio Hotel in Las Vegas. They have these wonderful fountains that erupt to music every half hour. The hundreds of geysers of water can be likened to writing qualities. We can choose six but chances are you will find six hundred if you look hard enough. (Full-size form is on page 235.)

Imagine each criterion is a geyser that shoots up according to the level or degree that trait is present in the piece of writing. After creating your trait fountain, have your students write about what they see in their writing.

Debriefing

What is the value of assessment? Does your trait fountain tell you anything about your writing? Was it hard to assess your writing? What difficulties did you encounter? Where are the strengths in your writing? What are the weaknesses?

FAULKNER FLUNKS: A SHORT HISTORY OF WRITING RUBRICS

I have to confess I am sick of rubrics. I don't think writing is bowling, so why score it as if it were? I do think it's good for students to have a common language to talk about writing craft and to have a sense of where any given piece succeeds and fails. I see a rubric, at best, as a simple tool for describing. That's why I like my writing trait fountain. I can see the profile of a piece of writing without having to pin down the exact level of achievement. Benchmarks invite direct comparisons, and though this may bear fruit for an evaluator, teaching writing is a much more complex activity. Let the test scorers at Measured Progress do that. It's their job. (Remember Lane's first truth of testing, page 183.) I can simply write a sentence or two that describes what my trait fountain shows. When I write about my writing, it forces me to use the language of the rubric without simply checking a box to denote the level achieved. The goal of writing assessment is eloquence, not officiousness. In my narrative, I may also include things that are not on the standard rubric.

Example:

> This piece lacks details, but then again I was writing through the eyes of a nearly blind Neanderthal water-skier, so he doesn't see much detail.

I asked Vince at Measured Progress what it was like to score an unusual or exemplary piece of writing that does not seem to fit the mold. For example, what if the stylistic rebel William Faulkner took the writing test? He said that, in such a case, the scorer has to step back from the rubric and realize the piece might be different from the traditional beginning, middle, and end. Only an experienced scorer could do this well.

Maja Wilson

Instead of fitting the rubric into the writing, the scorer must fit the writing into the rubric. It might force him to rethink the rubric.

Maja Wilson says, "A great piece of writing throws a writing assessment rubric into chaos." She is a high school teacher from Ludington, Michigan, who became so frustrated with having to assess her student Krystal's brilliant paper with a writing rubric that she wrote a whole book to figure out where rubrics came from and why they don't always serve the needs of writing teachers. The book is called *Rethinking Rubrics in Writing Assessment,* and it traces the history of writing rubrics from the laboratory of Paul Diederich of the Educational Testing Service in the early '60s to the 21st-century classroom.

Diederich was frustrated with the huge disparity in how evaluators scored college-entrance essays. He felt that what was needed was a more standardized method to weed out the inferior writers. With the G.I. Bill and federal loans and grants still intact, many more American students were trying to go to college, and Diederich and others sought a reliable means of ranking and sorting them.

Wilson questions if a tool created to eliminate and exclude serves the needs of teachers whose job it is to nurture and include. Her eloquent book should be studied by teachers who are ready to move beyond rubrics to a more personal form of writing assessment.

ELEGANT REBELLION

I sat in the room, and they handed me the blue test booklet. I was 19 years old, and this was my first official writing test. If I passed, I could get out of the second semester of freshman English, a class I detested. I opened the book and there was the test question staring me down. *Write about an embarrassing moment in your life. You have 45 minutes.*

An embarrassing moment, hmm. I was 19 years old, taking a stupid test to be read by God knows who. Did I want to share an embarrassing moment? I don't think so. I sat there for five minutes without writing one word. I contemplated just walking out and enduring another semester of the dreaded freshman English class. Then I got an idea. It came to me like a bolt of lightning through the musty room: I wonder if they care whether it's true or not!

Suddenly the haze lifted. I could write about whatever I wanted to write about and they would have to assess it on the writing, not the content. Embarrassing, let's see. I can do embarrassing. Hmm. Taking a bath in front of the entire high school during a pep rally. That would be pretty embarrassing. I began.

"They rolled the steaming bathtub across the wooden gymnasium floor as the crowd roared, 'Barrry, Barrrry'!"

I was pacing back and forth in my terry-cloth bathrobe. "Should I go out there? Could I go out there? What was I trying to prove?"

Within a few minutes I could not stop writing. I filled the eight pages with this one moment, and when it was time to end, the proctor had to wrench the book out of my hand. I was on a roll.

Now, you are wondering, did I pass the test? The answer is yes. But beyond passing the test, when I was on line for registration, I saw my freshman English professor elbowing his colleague and pointing at me. "That's him," I heard him say. "That's Barry Lane. That's the bath guy."

You see, not only did I pass that test, but I also gained literary distinction from my rebellious essay.

At the beginning of this chapter, I talked about the zombie essay and the elegant refusals that sometimes get the highest scores on writing tests. Talk to your students about the option of taking this route. Explain to them that the scorers don't care whether it's true or not. Let their imaginations fill the gap and write the kind of papers that will get the test scorers fired, because they won't be able to resist talking about them on their coffee break.

"YEAH, BUT . . ."

Readers' Questions Answered

What about grades? How do we grade writing so it helps students?

In my first book on writing for teachers, *After THE END: Teaching and Learning Creative Revision*, I addressed this issue by recounting a story told to me by Karl Diller, my linguistics professor at the University of New Hampshire. Diller had taken a course at Harvard with the legendary behaviorist B. F. Skinner, and he told me that for grades, Skinner gave only A's and incompletes. He reckoned all other grades promoted negative reinforcement. Grades also promote ambition, panic, competition, self-degradation, and feelings of inadequacy, to name only a few negative outcomes.

If you must use letter grades, see if you can grade a body of work or your students' coursework as a whole. You can start by giving all your students an A. You might tell them: "This is the good news. The bad news is this is what you have to do to keep it!" Create a meaningful rubric that suggests enjoyable, helpful activities such as these:

- Shows evidence of reading 30 minutes per night

- Writes 30 minutes per night

- Participates in class discussions

This way, grading reflects students' effort as much as their accomplishments. Include students' ability to self-assess as part of their grade as well. This lets them know you care about their ability to know their own work, a skill essential to a developing writer.

Recognize that students cannot take a detached view of grades, and that the simple act of receiving a grade can change their perception of themselves and even their physiology. It can turn some kids into rebels and others into self-loathing time bombs. I recently visited an elementary school where they carved the names of all the A students into bricks by the flagpole. One student, a fifth grader, had two bricks. The first was his "A student" brick and the second was his "In Memorium" brick. He had taken his own life on the night of report card day. His last words to his mother were, "With grades like these, I will never get into law school." It disturbed me that the principal at this school seemed to feel no personal culpability for the death of this child. What's more, his death didn't seem to suggest to her that the walk of fame and what it stood for might not send the right message to kids. But then again, the principal had described herself as an "A" student who had pulled herself up from poverty to this position as a leader of the school. To cast doubt on this system of rewards and punishment would be to cast doubt on her own personal identity. Great teachers protect their students from the injuries that grades bring. They focus on the child, not the achievement.

Do rubrics really work?

Sort of . . . not really is my latest answer to this question. Fifteen years ago, when I helped design Vermont's first rubric for portfolios, I would have had no doubt—of course, rubrics work. And what's more, they help teachers to agree on what's good in a piece of writing and what needs work. I can share with you the exact moment I began to doubt the authority of writing rubrics. A piece of writing from a fourth grader was benchmarked the lowest in organization, yet each time I read it, I delighted in the complexity and beauty and would not suggest the writer organize it any other way. Yet I could see exactly why it was scored so low. In fact, it almost seemed as if the writer was trying to get the lowest possible score in organization, yet the piece was complete. The student had described the American Dream as masterfully as Arthur Miller, and yet I was about to say it was poorly organized. Here it is. How would you score it in organization?

Looking for Treasure

I'm looking for treasure.
It's a lot of fun.
It's not a poem.
What you gonna do with that gun?

I'm gonna shoot some sharks
And snakes for bait
To bring me where to celebrate
With the treasure in my hand
With a rock'n roll band.

I won the race
And now I'm rich.
I got a mansion on a hill
And 3 boys and 2 girls.

How can we get away from the "have-tos" in writing? We have to have checklists. We have to use rubrics. We have to do four blocks. We have to use the same language. We have to all teach writing the same way!

Like most educational movements in America, the standards movements is simply a fad that has grown to enormous proportions, fueled by money and support from the federal government. It was a perfect storm that began with the *A Nation at Risk* report in 1983 and ended with the bipartisan-funded No Child Left Behind Act of 2001 that mandated adequate yearly progress of each public school in the country and testing at certain grade levels. Standardization and consistency are the hallmarks of this movement, and many textbook and testing companies have reeled in enormous profits. To learn more about this movement, read Susan Ohanian's *One Size Fits Few: The Folly of Educational Standards.*

Uncle Irwin

A few years after the law was passed, I was in Maine. It was the day after the U.S. Secretary of Education at that time, Rod Paige, had visited a school district there. He was greatly disappointed that students in classes were all reading different novels. According to the teacher I spoke with, he felt they should have been reading textbooks and they should have all been on the same page.

Instead of encouraging and developing teachers to be the best they can be, the standards movement has made consistency and data-driven progress the main goal. Benchmarks, rubrics, and checklists are now the norm in classrooms. On their own, these are not so bad. But the goal of making all teachers agree on exactly the same methods of teaching is simply counterproductive to a vibrant educational experience. I love it when teachers disagree and flaunt their biases. Isn't that what makes education interesting? Isn't that what makes people interesting? Isn't it great that we aren't all the same? Isn't that what students delight in as well?

This is my uncle, Irwin Flescher. For 30 years he was a school psychologist. Back in 1972, he wrote *Children in the Learning Factory: The Search for a Humanizing Teacher.*

My uncle's book began with one of his light verse poems, describing the state of American schools.

Schools teach facts,
and the facts are these:
schools are learning factories.

Jobs for all
in industry—
but work is all compulsory.

Children work
in the mental works—
wages are grades and mental quirks.

Teachers urge
to become exacter—
each boss is a crucial *fact*or.

Facts are drilled
by mechanical toys—
manu*fact*ured girls and boys.

Children learn,
it's a fact, you see—
children "learn" in a *fact*ory.

Uncle Irwin says that the only way we escape this conundrum is to be a humanizing teacher, a "High Priestess of Education." Thirty-five years later, Uncle Irwin's words still apply all too well to American education. Though there has been some progress, the factory model still persists. In fact, this book, long out of print, could be republished tomorrow with a new foreword by Jonathan Kozol. The system will only change when the leaders wake up to what real education is.

Till then, what can we do? I suggest elegant rebellion. Be the best teacher you can be. Remember who you are and why you are a teacher. Bring your passion into the classroom. When faced with monolithic programs, be eclectic. Choose what works for you and hurl the rest. Cast out the phony lessons in your midst. Make room for real thinking and writing and reading in your classroom. Be the best, most passionate, loving, caring, creative, tough, humanizing teacher you can be. Be a high priest or priestess of "real" education. Be the most glorious teacher you can be.

RETURN TO THE PENCIL PLANET

I can tell you the exact moment I became a writer. It was fourth grade, 1964. Miss Carolyn Foley stands at the front of the class wearing that familiar green dress that drapes her stately frame. She holds a picture clipping from a magazine in her hand and moves to the blackboard. Her high-heeled shoes make clicking sounds on the dark tile floor as we sit there at our school desks in anticipation.

"Today we are going to try something different," she says, emphasis on the word *different*. "We are going to write with our imagination. We are going to let our imagination carry our words. You might not know what that means yet, but that doesn't matter. You will find out when you start to write."

She pins the picture to the bulletin board and steps back like an artist trying to gain perspective. "Look at this photograph and let your imagination find the words to describe what you see. Write a story about the picture. Don't worry about your spelling or your grammar at first. You can fix that later. Don't let it make you lose your train of thought."

She moved away from the bulletin board and beckoned us to leave our seats and look at the photo, one row at a time. When my turn came, I stood there for a good ten minutes staring at the photo of the little pink elephant with the worried look on its face, standing in a forest of yellow pencils with their pink erasers thrusting into the deep blue sky. "What will I write about?" I thought, as I sat back at my desk. By now all my classmates had begun scribbling away on the paper, the distinct sound of lead scraping paper in stereo all around me. Each scrape seemed to sharpen my sense of failure. What were they writing about, I wondered? I thought for a moment and I remembered Miss Foley's words, "Let your imagination carry your words."

Suddenly it came to me: I could just make up a story about the little elephant and how he got to this place. I didn't have to tell a real story. There was no right answer here. The first sentence leapt onto the page before I was conscious of picking up the pencil.

"Once upon a time there was an elephant who had forgotten who he was, because, of course, elephants are very forgetful."

In the story, the elephant thinks he is a person and gets ridiculed by the people around him for the way he looks and the way he continues to break furniture when he sits on it. He is eventually helped by a kind doctor who tells him there is a place he can go to find his stories. The place is called the pencil planet and you go there to write the stories that tell you who you are. The elephant goes to the planet and learns to write with his trunk, creates a land where creatures like him live, and makes many friends. He gets to live inside the stories he creates, and for the first time in this life he is not alone.

All of the students in the class had finished their stories in the 20 minutes before recess. My story was complete a month later. Miss Foley gave me special permission to take it home and make a book out of it. I remember staying up late at night, pacing back and forth in my bathrobe like the young Flaubert, musing about my story. "What would happen next? How would I end it? Should there be a sequel?" I made carefully colored illustrations and borrowed my mother's stapler to make the book. When I brought it into class, Miss Foley held it up for all to see and read it slowly, with deep emotion. Soon, I had a small cult following in the back of the room. They would ask me when my next book was coming out. What was it going to be about? There was no doubt in my mind now—I was a writer.

Looking back, I realize my story about the elephant was really about me. My parents were second-generation immigrant Jews who had spent much of their childhood rejecting the Old World values of their parents and moving into mainstream American society. My father had changed his name from Zysblatt to Lane to give it a slightly more Anglo sound. He had grown up in great poverty in the tenements of the Lower East Side of Manhattan and ended up taking his family to Dover, New Hampshire, on the coattails of the company he worked for. Being one of only a few Jewish children in a public school where the Christian religion was openly practiced added to my feeling of alienation. Miss Foley sensed this, and asked me to tell the story of Chanukah to the class and make a papier-mâché dreidel from a Dixie cup while all the rest of the class was making Josephs and Marys for the creche. She knew that writing was not only an academic skill but an essential tool for self-expression. She nurtured our sense of self through our writing and, like the elephant in my story, I gained acceptance.

Here is a photo of Miss Foley, circa 1960. Sometimes I hold it up at my writing seminars and ask the teachers who attend to think of their great writing teachers. You know who I mean, the teacher who saw you for who you were or the teachers who held a high standard and taught with passion and clarity. I tell them one of my favorite stories about Miss Foley. She once wrote a reading grant and bought guitars for every student in her class. The name of the grant was "Guitars with Strings Attached" and she made the case that reading the chords G, D, A, and F was decoding. For 28 years, she got to school a half hour early and tuned guitars. She taught every student in her class to play the old folk song "Tom Dooley" on the guitar.

Miss Foley, circa 1960

Sometimes I stop at this point in the story and I turn to the room of teachers of all grade levels and subjects. I ask them, "Could you do this in today's classroom with all the demands placed on teachers from above?" Most of the heads shake no in an almost spring-loaded reflex. Only a few veteran teachers in the back give a slight affirmative nod, not wanting to tip their hand. These are the teachers who sit in the back row at staff meetings, that Mona Lisa smile planted firmly on their faces whenever new meaningless directives are handed down from above. These are the teachers who will do right for their students no matter what they are told to do from above.

Then I ask a second question. "How many of you think you could do more than you are doing to bring your passion and your self into the classroom?" Then the nods come almost in unison. Every teacher has a Miss Foley inside, waiting to emerge.

Seven years ago, I went back to visit Miss Foley in her house on Silver Street in Dover, New Hampshire. I knew exactly where she lived because we had gone there for a field trip once to look at her bird feeders. We marched over there singing World War I songs. "Over hill, over dale, we have hit the dusty trail as those caissons go rolling along . . . ."

Like many people, I had passed her house many times over the years on visits to my parents, and occasionally I would think about trying to visit, but I never did. Now, I walked up the familiar long brick walkway to the front door. I knocked and like magic she appeared. At first, I thought she was a lot shorter. Then I remembered I was only four feet tall in the fourth grade. Her hair had turned gray, and there were more wrinkles, but those eyes sparkled with the same passion.

Me in fourth grade

"Do you remember me?" I asked (perhaps the teacher's worst nightmare scenario), but she did. "Barry" was the only word she said as we embraced.

Later, I found out that not only did she remember me, she remembered exactly where I sat: "right next to my desk." As we sat in her living room sipping cranberry juice, I tried to tell her what she meant to me. I shared a memory with her of one morning, near the beginning of the school year, before I wrote "Return to the Pencil Planet." I remember thinking that if I could write small enough and faint enough, my penmanship might appear neat because the entire page would be blank. I sharpened a few pencils and assumed my medieval-scribe writing position, hunched over my wooden desk. Miss Foley was making her rounds. I felt her hand gently touch my shoulder and she said, "Barry, what happened to your wonderful, looping letters?" I exhaled deeply and began to write in my normal fashion. Later I would reflect that this was perhaps the only time in school I remember a teacher saying, "It's okay to be the way you are already; you don't just have to squeeze yourself into a little box to survive. "

When I told my story, Miss Foley paused and said, " Barry, I have a confession to make to you. You know how you would see this beautiful handwriting on the blackboard? I would get into school early, draw staff lines across the blackboard and then erase the little lines so the principal would think I had great hand-writing, too."

Like all the great ones in education, be they teachers or administrators, Miss Foley did not pass down the anxiety she felt from above to her students. She knew how to create a safe zone for learning. She didn't follow the curriculum. The curriculum followed her.

This is a book about how to teach writing, and I have written it for any teacher at any grade level or subject, drawing on my many years of experience working with students of all ages and all grade levels and subject areas. But along with learning how to teach writing, it is important to remember why we teach writing. Some might argue that we teach writing to create better workers who can communicate ideas with precision, depth, and clarity. Others might say it's to succeed on writing tests that measure student and school successes. Still others might say it is so we can be productive citizens and contribute to our democratic way of life. All true, perhaps, but as we explore our own journey back to the Pencil Planet, I think of the inscription at the temple of the Greek god Apollo in Delphi: "Know thyself."

We teach writing to help ourselves and our students find out who we are.

Me and Miss Foley at the 6th annual Miss Foley Day 2007

LANE'S TOP 21 FORMS

Here are Lane's Top 21 Forms to keep a writer's workshop organized. I have divided them into two categories. The first set of forms helps students keep track of it all; the second helps the teacher do the same. (See pages 212–233 or www.scholastic.com for full-sized forms.)

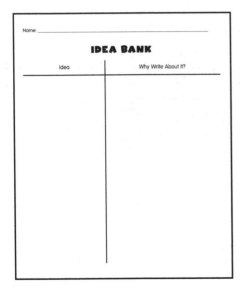

Idea Banks
Banks help you save money. Idea banks help you save ideas. This form can be handed to students or used as a lesson to do a class brainstorm of ideas to write about. (see page 212)

Writing Folder Cover Sheet
Students can manage their own writing folders. A sheet like this can be like a running table of contents that helps students feel a sense of accomplishment about the wad of papers crammed into their folders.

Name: _____ **Date:** _____

STUDENT READING/WRITING GENRE CHART

Writing Genre	Reading Genre
Total Writing Genre _____	Total Reading Genre _____

Student Reading/Writing Genre Chart
Use this form to teach your students how to keep track of writing and reading genres. Take time to marvel at all the different genres you encounter when you read and write freely.

Name: _____ **Date:** _____

STUDENT WRITING GOALS FOR THE WEEK

"If you wish to be a writer, write." —Epictetus

Monday	
Tuesday	
Wednesday	
Thursday	
Friday	

What happened this week?

Student Writing Goals for the Week
Students need their own "to-do" lists. This will help them stay in control of their work and focus their activities during writing time.

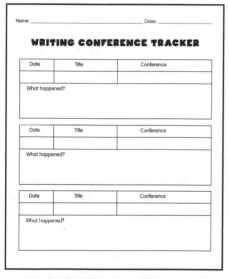

Name: _____ **Class:** _____

WRITING CONFERENCE TRACKER

Date	Title	Conference

What happened?

Date	Title	Conference

What happened?

Date	Title	Conference

What happened?

Writing Conference Tracker
This form is attached to a piece of writing. It tracks the conferences a student has had with students and/or the teacher. It is a mini-history of discussion about a piece of writing. Good conferences evaporate as fast as bad ones. Students need a written reminder of what happened. This form helps a writer take away something from each conference. It can be used to begin a discussion at a student-teacher conference.

Name: _____ **Class:** _____

WHAT I LEARNED FROM LITERATURE

Date	Title	Genre	What I Learned

What I Learned From Literature
Here students take a minute after or while reading a book to scribble a note about what they learned from it.

Name: _____ Date: _____

WRITING REFLECTION SHEET

Piece:

What sticks with you:

I wonder:

One thing a writer will do:

Writing Reflection Sheet

Here is my favorite reflection sheet. Use it for a first full-group writing workshop or small-group conference. The first two sections are filled out by the readers and the last by the writer at the end of the conference.

Name: _____ Date: _____

DO-IT-YOURSELF TEACHER CONFERENCE

Your teacher is too busy to meet with you today but you really need a conference. What will you do? Easy! Pretend you are meeting. Write a play of what you will say to each other.

Title: _____

Me:

Teacher:

Me:

Teacher:

Me:

Teacher:

Me:

Teacher:

Do-It-Yourself Teacher Conference

Here is a chance for your students to show you what a nag you have become. They write a short play about a fictional writing conference with you. With any luck, they will say exactly what you would have said.

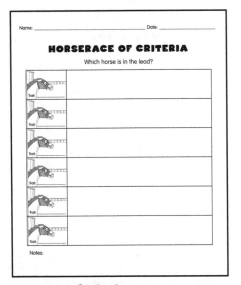

Name: _____ Date: _____

HORSERACE OF CRITERIA

Which horse is in the lead?

Trait:

Trait:

Trait:

Trait:

Trait:

Trait:

Notes:

Horserace of Criteria

This is where you put writing traits used for assessment in the starting gate. Students draw a crayon line across the page to show which traits are in the lead. At the bottom, in the note section, they write a brief note about what the race shows about their writing.

Name: _____ Date: _____

MY GRAMMAR REPORT CARD

What I know:

What I am working on:

Proof Box

My Grammar Report Card

Here is a chance for students to take ownership of the grammar they have learned and want to learn. Students can fill out their grammar report cards each quarter. Students also get to focus on what they want to learn more about. In the "proof box" they write a sentence or two that demonstrates the concept they have learned.

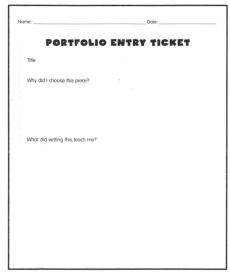

Name: _____ Date: _____

PORTFOLIO ENTRY TICKET

Title:

Why did I choose this piece?

What did writing this teach me?

Name: _____ Date: _____

STUDENT QUARTERLY EVALUATION

What does someone have to do to be a good writer?

What is your best piece of writing this quarter?

What makes it best?

What is your least effective piece this quarter? Why?

How have you improved?

What are your goals for next term?

Portfolio Entry Ticket

This is a form students fill out when they decide to move a piece from their writing folder and put it in their portfolio (a collection of their best work).

Student Quarterly Evaluation

Here is a quick reflection form for your students to fill out at the end of a term.

WHERE ARE YOU TODAY?

Name	M	T	W	Th	F

TEACHER YEARLY MINI-LESSON PLANNER

	Week 1	Week 2	Week 3	Week 4
September				
October				
November				
December				
January				
February				
March				
April				
May				
June				
July				
August				

Where Are You Today?

Here is a quick check-in sheet for you to use on your clipboard. It will tell you where each student is in her or his writing each day. You can also have students pass this sheet around on a clipboard. Or, create a larger version of this form on a bulletin board.

Teacher Yearly Mini-Lesson Planner

Here is a chance for you to reflect on what you observe in your students' writing and then decide on the lessons you want to plan for them throughout the year. This is a big-picture lesson planner. I suggest you plan the whole year in August and keep this in a separate place. Revise this plan throughout the year as you teach lessons in response to your students' needs. In December, check this original plan to determine what lessons you have not yet taught. This will help you make a new plan for the spring.

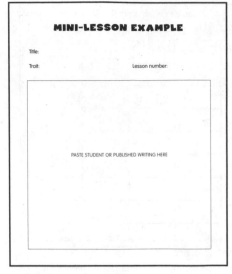

MINI-LESSON PLANNER

Title and lesson number:

Point:

Examples:

Questions to ask students:

What happened:

Mini-Lesson Planner

Here is a simple form for you to plan a mini-lesson. Copy it and create your own file of mini-lessons. Label and attach a blank page labeled "Example" where you paste a writing sample that will help you teach the lesson.

MINI-LESSON EXAMPLE

Title:

Trait: Lesson number:

PASTE STUDENT OR PUBLISHED WRITING HERE

Mini-Lesson Example

Collect your favorite writing samples from students and published literature to use in mini-lessons. Cut and paste these examples onto this sheet. If you photocopy this onto cardstock, you can create your own big deck of mini-lesson cards over time.

WRITING BLOCK PLANNER

Date:

Mini-lesson:

Meet with:

Work on:

Notes:

Writing Block Planner

Here you have a planner for each writing block.

TRAIN A CRITIC TODAY

When they say . . .	You say . . .
I liked it.	What part?
It was okay.	Tell me what's okay and what is not okay
It was boring.	Tell me the most boring part.
I could identify with it.	What parts? Why?
I love it.	Could you repeat that?

Train a Critic Today

Use this sheet to talk your students about how to train one another to be better peer critics.

ASSESS ANYTHING

Trait:	Assessing:		
	1	2	3

Assess Anything

Assess anything from tortilla chips to bubble gum to school lunches. Create criteria and descriptors for three levels of achievement. Teach your students that assessing is describing, not ranking.

Name: _____ Date: _____

QUARTERLY EVALUATION

What can _____ do as a writer?

Goals for next quarter:

Quarterly Evaluation

Here is a simple anecdotal assessment of each student in your class. Simple forms like this provide a chance for both teacher and student to reflect on where they have been and where they are going.

GRADING RUBRIC PLANNER

A Students show evidence of . . .

B Students show evidence of . . .

C Students show evidence of . . .

D Students show evidence of . . .

Grading Rubric Planner

If you must grade each quarter, make sure that you consider a student's effort and progress along with the finished product. A simple grading rubric planner like this one allows you to say, for example:

- *An "A" student shows evidence of reading 30 minutes per night; an A student writes regularly and revises at least two pieces per quarter.*

- *A "B" student shows evidence of frequently reading 30 minutes a night.*

- *A "C" student shows evidence of sometimes reading 30 minutes per night.*

- *A "D" student shows evidence of rarely reading 30 minutes per night.*

Name: _____

IDEA BANK

Idea	Why Write About It?

But How Do You Teach Writing? © 2008 Barry Lane   Scholastic Professional

Name: _____ Class: _____

WRITING FOLDER COVER SHEET

Date	Title	Draft	Genre

Name: _____   Date: _____

STUDENT READING/WRITING GENRE CHART

Writing Genre	Reading Genre

Total Writing Genre

_____

Total Reading Genre

_____

Name: _____ Date: _____

STUDENT WRITING GOALS FOR THE WEEK

"If you wish to be a writer, write." —Epictetus

Monday	
Tuesday	
Wednesday	
Thursday	
Friday	

What happened this week?

Name: _____ Class: _____

WRITING CONFERENCE TRACKER

Date	Title	Conference

What happened?

Date	Title	Conference

What happened?

Date	Title	Conference

What happened?

But How Do You Teach Writing? © 2008 Barry Lane   Scholastic Professional

Name: _____ Class: _____

WHAT I LEARNED FROM LITERATURE

Date	Title	Genre	What I Learned

WRITING REFLECTION SHEET

Piece:

What sticks with you:

I wonder:

One thing a writer will do:

DO-IT-YOURSELF
TEACHER CONFERENCE

Your teacher is too busy to meet with you today, but you really need a conference. What will you do? Easy! Pretend you are meeting. Write a play of what you will say to each other.

Title: _____

Me:

Teacher:

Me:

Teacher:

Me:

Teacher:

Me:

Teacher:

HORSERACE OF CRITERIA

Which horse is in the lead?

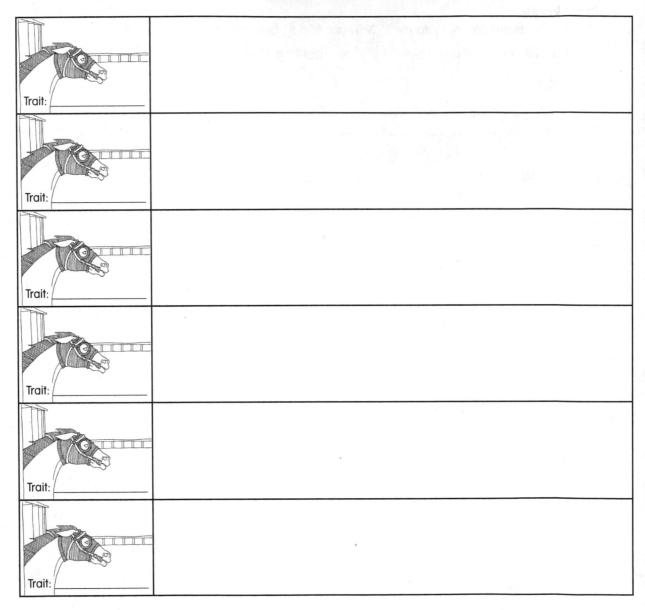

Trait: _____

Trait: _____

Trait: _____

Trait: _____

Trait: _____

Trait: _____

Notes:

Name: _____ Date: _____

MY GRAMMAR REPORT CARD

What I know:

What I am working on:

Proof Box

PORTFOLIO ENTRY TICKET

Title:

Why did I choose this piece?

What did writing this teach me?

But How Do You Teach Writing? © 2008 Barry Lane   Scholastic Professional

Name: _____ Date: _____

STUDENT QUARTERLY EVALUATION

What does someone have to do to be a good writer?

What is your best piece of writing this quarter?

What makes it best?

What is your least effective piece this quarter? Why?

How have you improved?

What are your goals for next term?

WHERE ARE YOU TODAY?

Name	M	T	W	Th	F

TEACHER YEARL.
MINI-LESSON PLANNER

	Week 1	Week 2	Week 3	Week 4
September				
October				
November				
December				
January				
February				
March				
April				
May				
June				
July				
August				

MINI-LESSON PLANNER

Title and lesson number:

Point:

Examples:

Questions to ask students:

What happened:

But How Do You Teach Writing? © 2008 Barry Lane   Scholastic Professional

MINI-LESSON EXAMPLE

Title:

Trait: Lesson number:

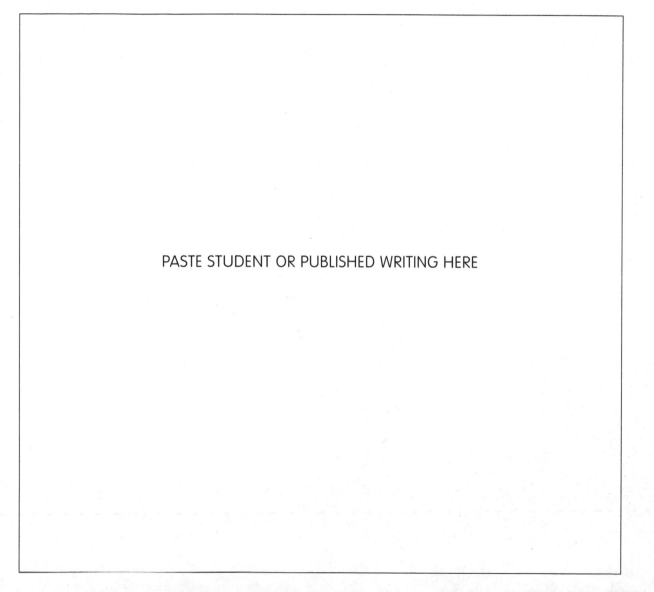

PASTE STUDENT OR PUBLISHED WRITING HERE

WRITING BLOCK PLANNER

Date:

Mini-lesson:

Meet with:

Work on:

Notes:

TRAIN A CRITIC TODAY

When they say . . .	You say . . .
I liked it.	What part?
It was okay.	Tell me what's okay and what is not okay
It was boring.	Tell me the most boring part.
I could identify with it.	What parts? Why?
I love it.	Could you repeat that?

ASSESS ANYTHING

Trait:	Assessing:		
	1	2	3

Name: _____ Date: _____

QUARTERLY EVALUATION

What can _____ do as a writer?

Goals for next quarter:

GRADING RUBRIC PLANNER

 A Students show evidence of . . .

 B Students show evidence of . . .

 C Students show evidence of . . .

 D Students show evidence of . . .

THE THREE-ACT STORY

Character _____

Trouble _____

Dream _____

Obstacle

Act 1 _____

Act 2 _____

Act 3 _____

Obstacle

Obstacle

Obstacle

1. Set-up

2. Mix-up

3. End-up

GENRE LIST

Here is a list of some possible writing genres.

Acceptance speech	Elegy	Love letter	Radio spot
Ad copy	E-mail	Lullaby	Rap
Address to jury	Encyclopedia article	Magazine article	Recipe
Advice column	Epilogue	Manifesto	Recipe poem
Allegory	Epitaph	Manual	Recommendation
Apology	Essay	Map	Restaurant review
Autobiography	Eulogy	Memorandum	Resume
Billboard	Experiment	Memorial plaque	Riddle
Biography	Expose	Menu	Rock opera
Birth announcement	Fable	Minutes	Sales letter
Blueprint	Family history	Monologue	Schedule
Book review	Fashion show monologue	Movie review	Screenplay
Brochure	Flyer	Myth	Sermon
Bumper sticker	Foreword	Nature guide	Sign
Business letter	Fortune cookie insert	News story	Slogan
Bylaws	Found poem	Newsletter	Song lyric
Campaign ad	Graduation speech	Nomination speech	Spell
Campaign speech	Graffiti	Nonsense rhyme	Sports story
Cartoon	Greeting card	Nursery rhyme	Storyboard
Chant poem	Haiku	Obituary	Survey
Chat room log	Headline	Oracle	Tall tale
Cheer	Horoscope	Packaging copy	Test
Children's story	Infomercial	Parable	Thank-you note
Classified ad	Instructions	Petition	Theater review
Comic strip	Insult poem	Play	Toast
Consumer report	Interview	Poem	To-do list
Daydream	Invitation	Police report	Tour guide speech
Death certificate	Jingle	Post card	Translation
Debate	Joke	PowerPoint presentation	Treaty
Dialogue	Journal entry	Prayer	T-shirt design
Diary	Keynote address	Precis	TV spot
Diatribe	Law	Prediction	Want ad
Dictionary entry	Letter of complaint	Preface	Warrant
Directions	Letter to the editor	Profile	Wedding vows
Dream analysis	Letter of request	Prologue	
Editorial	Limerick	Public service announcement	

Adapted from a similar list in Why We Must Run With Scissors, *Discover Writing Press 2002. Used with permission, www.discoverwriting.com*

BARRY'S FAVORITE RUBRIC

Place trait of writing in box and show the level present in a piece by how high you draw your line for each trait.

A YEAR OF WRITING

Here is a quick overview of what a year in writing workshop might look like:

AUGUST
Get it going

- This is the time to get the routines going. Get students doing regular writing on topics of choice.
- Encourage head scratching and pimple time.
- Create lists and lists of stuff to write about.
- Encourage exploratory writing in the notebook.
- Get sharing rituals going.

SEPTEMBER
Establish writing routines

- Establish writing time, conferring time, sharing time.
- Establish mini-lesson time:
- Present genre experiments to your students, including wacky we-search.
- Prod students with ideas of what to write about.
- Publish at least one small piece of writing as a motivation.

OCTOBER
Kick it up a notch

- Introduce genre and lessons on craft revision.
- Encourage students to set writing goals.
- Start looking in your writer's notebook for stuff to write about.

NOVEMBER
Celebrate and give thanks

- Thanksgiving is a great time to create a mini-literary festival.
- Sponsor a Day of Sharing.
- Students finish one piece to read at the festival, solidifying your students' sense of audience.
- Invite parents or make it just a classroom event.

DECEMBER
Wind down

- Have students move their best work this term from folders to portfolios.
- Students write a letter of reflection about their work so far and a projection of what they want to do.

JANUARY
A new dawn

- Here's a great time to shift gears. Ask students to look at their December reflections and decide where they want to head in the spring.
- If you want to introduce research writing, now is a good time.
- January can serve as an interlude between the fall writing workshop and the spring one.

FEBRUARY
Nonfiction writing workshop: test essays

- Here is a good time to play with research and essay writing.
- Most state testing is in March so here is a chance to complete some lessons on crafting a prompt response.
- Have students finish a piece of writing by the end of the month.
- This is also a good time for introducing wacky we-search.

MARCH
Literary festival month

- March is a tough month. In some states there is a week's vacation. In New England, it's a long battle to the end of winter. To make it worse, testing breaks up the class's rhythm.
- Create some kind of small literary celebration to offset the March Madness and the doldrums.

APRIL
Pause for poetry

- April is National Poetry Month and a great chance to explore a new genre as a group study.
- If you are exploring nonfiction writing, suggest writing poems about subjects you have researched, as well as poetry about all subjects.
- Make April a poetry oasis.

MAY
Portfolio reflection

- By May students should have a wealth of material to review.
- Take the time to have your students reflect on their writing.
- Have them pull a few pieces for their portfolio and write a letter of reflection about why they are their strongest samples.
- Also have your students reflect on what they have learned.

JUNE
Where are you going?
Where have you been?

- June is a great time to reflect on the year's achievement as a writer.
- Have students choose their favorite piece of writing and read it to the class.
- Ask them to write a year-end assessment.

REFERENCES

Allen. J. (1999). *Words, Words, Words: Teaching Vocabulary in Grades 4–12*. Portland, ME: Stenhouse

Anderson, C. (2000). *How's it going?: A practical guide to conferring with student writers.* Portsmouth, NH: Heinemann.

Anderson, J., & Spandel, V. (2005). *Mechanically inclined: Building grammar, usage, and style into writer's workshop.* Portland, ME: Stenhouse.

Ballenger, B. (2006). *The curious researcher: A guide to writing research papers.* London: Longman.

Ballenger, B. & Lane, B. (1996). *Discovering the writer within: 40 days to more imaginative writing.* Cincinnati, OH: Writer's Digest Books.

Barron, T. A. (2002). *The hero's trail: A guide for a heroic life.* New York: Puffin.

Bernabei, G. (2005). *Reviving the essay: How to teach structure without formula.* Shoreham, VT: Discover Writing Press.

Buckner, A. (2005). *Notebook know-how: Strategies for the writer's notebook.* Portland, ME: Stenhouse.

Campbell, C. (2007). *The giggly guide to grammar.* Shoreham, VT: Discover Writing Press.

Carroll, K. (2005). *Rules of the red rubber ball: Find and sustain your life's work.* New York: ESPN.

Cram, L. (1989). *Left Handed.* Middlebury, VT: Homegrown Books.

Culham, R. (2003). *6+1 traits of writing: The complete guide (Grades 3 and up).* New York: Scholastic

Dorfman, L., & Cappelli, R. (2007). *Mentor texts: Teaching writing through children's literature, K–6.* Portland, ME: Stenhouse.

Flescher, I. (1972). *Children in the learning factory: The search for a humanizing teacher.* Philadelphia, PA: Chilton Book Co.

Fletcher, R. (1996). *Breathing in, breathing out: Keeping a writer's notebook.* Portsmouth, NH: Heinemann.

Fletcher, R. (2003). *A writer's notebook: Unlocking the writer within you.* New York: HarperTrophy.

Fletcher, R. (2006). *Boy writers: Reclaiming their voices.* Portland, ME: Stenhouse.

Fletcher, R., & Portalupi, J. (2001). *Writing workshop: The essential guide.* Portsmouth, NH: Heinemann.

Fletcher, R., & Portalupi, J. (2005). *Lessons for the writer's notebook.* Portsmouth, NH: Heinemann.

Frank, A., & Mooyaart, B. M. (translation). (1993). *Anne Frank: The diary of a young girl.* New York: Bantam.

Friedman, T. (2007). *The world is flat.* New York: Picador.

Graves, D. (1983). *Writing: Teachers and children at work.* Portsmouth, NH: Heinemann.

Graves, D., & Kittle, P. (2005). *Inside writing: How to teach the details of craft.* Portsmouth, NH: Heinemann.

Glynn, C. (2001). *Learning on their feet: A sourcebook for kinesthetic learning across the curriculum K–8.* Shoreham, VT: Discover Learning Press.

Hewitt, G. (2005). *Hewitt's guide to slam poetry and poetry slam.* Shoreham, VT: Discover Writing Press.

Johnson, S. (2005). *Everything bad for you is good for you: How today's popular culture is actually making us smarter.* New York: Riverhead.

Kielburger, C., & Kielburger, M. (2006). *Me to we: Finding meaning in a material world.* New York: Fireside.

Laminack, L. (2007). *Cracking open the author's craft: Teaching the art of writing.* New York: Scholastic.

Lane, B., & Bernabei, G. (2001). *Why we must run with scissors: Voice lessons in persuasive writing, 3–12.* Gainesville, FL: Maupin Press.

Lane, B. (1992). *After the end: Teaching and learning creative revision.* Portsmouth, NH: Heinemann.

Lane, B. (1999). *Reviser's toolbox.* Shoreham, VT: Discover Writing Press.

Lane, B. (2002). *The tortoise and the hare continued. . . .* Shoreham, VT: Discover Writing Press.

Lane, B. (2003). *51 wacky we-search reports: Face the facts with fun.* Shoreham, VT: Discover Writing Press.

Lane, B. (2006). *Hooked on meaning: Writing craft video lessons that improve achievement on writing tests through authentic instruction, for students grade 3–8.* Shoreham, VT: Discover Writing Press.

Lane, B., & Young, R. (2008). *The non-fiction writers/readers toolbox.* Shoreham, VT: Discover Writing Press.

Levine, P. (1996). *The simple truth: Poems.* New York: Knopf.

Lyne, S. (2007). *Writing poetry from the inside out.* Naperville, IL: Sourcebooks, Inc.

Mandela, N. (1995). *Long walk to freedom: The autobiography of Nelson Mandela.* Boston, MA: Back Bay Books.

Moline, S. (1995). *I see what you mean: Children at work with visual information.* Portland, ME: Stenhouse.

Morris, A. (2005). *Vocabulary unplugged.* Shoreham, VT: Discover Writing Press.

Murray, D. (1989). *Expecting the unexpected: Teaching myself—and others—to read and write.* Portsmouth, NH: Boynton/Cook.

Murray, D. (2003). *A writer teaches writing revised.* Boston, MA: Houghton Mifflin.

Newkirk, T. (2005). *The school essay manifesto: Reclaiming the essay for students and teachers.* Shoreham, VT: Discover Writing Press.

Newkirk, T. (2002). *Misreading masculinity: Boys, literacy, and popular culture.* Portsmouth, NH: Heinemann.

Noden, H. (1999). *Image grammar.* Portsmouth, NH: Heinemann.

Ohanian, S. (1999). *One size fits few: The folly of educational standards.* Portsmouth, NH: Heinemann.

Orwell, G. (2003). *Shooting an elephant.* New York: Bantam.

Pink, D. (2005). *A whole new mind.* New York: Penguin.

Rief, L. (2007). *Seeking Diversity: Language Arts with Adolescents.* Portsmouth, NH: Heinemann.

Sagan, C. (1985). *Contact.* New York: Simon & Schuster.

Scheps, S. (2002). *Review of: Tortoise and the hare continued . . . .* Cambridge, MA: Cahners Business Information.

Seinfeld, J. (1994). *SeinLanguage.* New York: Bantam.

Shannon, P. (2007). *Reading against democracy: The broken promises of reading instruction.* Portsmouth, NH: Heinemann.

Smith, F. (1987). *Joining the literacy club: Further essays into education.* Portsmouth, NH: Heinemann.

Spandel, V. (2004). *Creating writers through 6-trait writing assessment and instruction.* Boston: Pearson Education Inc.

Strunk, W., White, E. B., & R. Angell. (1999). *The elements of style.* 4th Ed. Boston: Allyn & Bacon.

White, E. B. (2004). *Charlotte's web.* New York: HarperTrophy.

Wilson, M. (2006). *Rethinking rubrics in writing assessment.* Portsmouth, NH: Heinemann.